What People  Say About
Rock Your Feminine Type To Rock Your Business

If you are a woman who owns her own business—read this book! Joy's Feminine Type Success System shows you how to find your feminine type, your biz type and your superpowers. You will know precisely what to do to rock your business and massively monetize your mastery. This resource is practical, inspiring and brilliant. I love this book and highly recommend it.

~ Caterina Rando MCC
Thriving Business Coach and Speaker for Women
www.caterinarando.com

I can't tell you how much I love this book. It's clever, deep, energetic, loving, thoughtful, honest and LIFE CHANGING. Joy gives entrepreneurs critical information they need to clearly identify their unique feminine type and the feminine type of the people they serve—leading to having more successful businesses.

~ Blaze Lazarony
Entrepreneurial Business Strategist
www.blazeabrilliantpath.com

This book will revolutionize the way you see yourself as a women and as an entrepreneur. Joy is truly a magical, intuitive and powerful soul. She plugs right into your heart and essence, seeing your best, most authentic self.

~ Eyenie Schultz
Soul-Style Coaching at Technicolor Priestess
www.technicolorpriestess.com

Joy has created a masterpiece assessment tool that is invaluable in understanding more about who we are as women business owners. This is a must read for female entrepreneurs who want to attract more ideal clients, understand what makes them tick and be of greater service to them.

~ Julie Van De Wyngaerde
Empowerment Coach at Julie Unplugged
www.julieunplugged.com

Rock Your Feminine Type To Rock Your Business is spunky, clever, charming and original—a mirror of its author. Unlike other typing methods which mostly offer explanations of why you are the way you are, what is so wonderful about this book is Joy's sage advice on how to deal with the shadow side of being. She shows you exactly how to deal with what is tripping you up in your business and how making just a few, simple changes can have a profound impact on your business.

~ Nina Price
L.Ac. Acupuncturist and Midlife Reinvention Specialist
www.midlifewithoutcrisis.com

Rock Your Feminine Type To Rock Your Business is a potent tool for personal transformation and creating business success. Joy makes it easy to find your Feminine Type, activate your superpowers and embrace the shadow or challenges that we face. Joy's work is inspiring, innovative and on the leading edge of the women's empowerment movement. I would definitely recommend you read this to Rock your Feminine Powers in your Business!

~ Christel Arcucci, Soul Centered Prosperity Mentor
www.ChristelArcucci.com

Rock Your Feminine Type To Rock Your Business is a super fun treasure hunt that leads you to greater self-knowledge, a deeper understanding of why you struggle in business, and how to overcome those old patterns to experience success and abundance. Joy's packed this full of strategies, insight, and practical tools to help take things to the next level in your business ... and on your spiritual path as well.

~ Karen Hager
Intuitive Guide and host of Out of the Fog radio
www.karenhager.com

Rock Your Feminine Type To Rock Your Business

Discover Your Unique Feminine Power With The Feminine Type Success System

Joy Balma, MA, MS

Rock Your Feminine Type To Rock Your Business is written by Joy Balma

Copyright © 2014, Joy Balma

All rights reserved. This book may not be published, reproduced, transmitted, emailed, photocopied, scanned, or otherwise distributed or produced in any form without the prior written consent of the publisher except in the case of brief quotes in a credited review.

Library of Congress Control Number 2013922510

ISBN 9780991087099

Brilliant Living Press
P.O. Box 23323
Pleasant Hill, CA 94534

www.rockyourfemininetype.com
joy@rockyourfemininetype.com

Illustrations by Heather Davulcu
Book designed by e-book-design.com

Printed in the USA

Limit of Liability/ Disclaimer of Warranty

The stories contained within this book are based on real people but their names have been changed. This book does not claim that your results will be the same. The advice and strategies contained herein may not be suitable for your situation. Neither the publisher nor author shall be liable for any loss of profit or any commercial damages, including but not limited to special, incidental, consequential, or other damages.

Dedication

I dedicate this book to my parents Jayne and Mike, who have always given me roots with wings to soar.

Acknowledgments

There are some very special people I would like to thank for contributing to the creation of this book. To my friends Allie and DRK, whose steadfast and generous support helped this book become a reality. I am grateful for my editor Lynda McDaniel, whose enthusiasm for this book in the early stages inspired me to keep writing. Heather Davulcu worked tirelessly to bring the Feminine Types to life with her illustrations. A special thanks to my coaching colleagues Blaze Lazarony and Eyenie Schultz who read early versions of my manuscript and extended their feedback and suggestions. To all my coaching clients who gave me permission to use their stories and who have contributed to my understanding of Feminine Types in business—I am grateful for all of you.

Table of Contents

Introduction 1
1 ~ Who Put This Elephant in My Business? 5
2 ~ Follow The Yellow Brick Road 11
3 ~ The Good Girl's Handbook 17
4 ~ What's Success Got to Do With It? 23
5 ~ Your Girl Power 27
    The Feminine Type Questionnaire. 31
6 ~ You've Got Superpowers! 39
7 ~ Every Queen Rules Her World 45
    The 4 Biz Types 46
        The Nurturers 51
        The Experts. 55
        The Creatives. 59
        The Leaders. 63
    Putting It All Together 67
    Your Feminine Type Profile 68
8 ~ The Feminine Type Success System 69
    Step Into Your Highest Potential. 71
    The Feminine Type Success System Chart. 73
9 ~ Turn Your Shadow Into Your Light 75
    Your Feminine Type Shadow 77
    Your Biz Type Shadow 79
10 ~ The Eight Feminine Types 91
11 ~ The Nurturer Biz Types 95

The Loyal SWEETHEART 97
    Quick Look 98
    Who's That Girl? 98
    The Elephant In Your Business 100
    Inspirations for THE SWEETHEART 104
    Wake Up Your Inner SWEETHEART 105

The Nurturing SAINT 107
    Quick Look 108
    Who's That Girl? 108
    The Elephant In Your Business 110
    Inspirations for THE SAINT. 115
    Wake Up Your Inner SAINT 116

12 ~ The Expert Biz Types 117
  The Responsible EXCELLENCE GIRL 119
    Quick Look 120
    Who's That Girl? 120
    The Elephant In Your Business 121
    Inspirations for THE EXCELLENCE GIRL. 126
    Wake Up Your Inner EXCELLENCE GIRL. 127

  The Knowledgeable GODDESS GEEK 129
    Quick Look 130
    Who's That Girl? 130
    The Elephant In Your Business 132
    Inspirations for THE GODDESS GEEK 135
    Wake Up Your Inner GODDESS GEEK 136

13 ~ The Creative Biz Types 137
  The Creative MUSE 139
    Quick Look 140
    Who's That Girl? 140
    The Elephant In Your Business 142
    Inspirations for THE MUSE 146
    Wake Up Your Inner MUSE 147

>
> **The Free-Spirited SEEKER** 149
>> Quick Look 150
>> Who's That Girl? 150
>> The Elephant In Your Business 153
>> Inspirations for THE SEEKER 155
>> Wake Up Your Inner SEEKER 156

14 ~ The Leader Biz Types 157
> **The Ambitious SUCCESS GIRL** 159
>> Quick Look 160
>> Who's That Girl? 160
>> The Elephant In Your Business 162
>> Inspirations for THE SUCCESS GIRL 166
>> Wake Up Your Inner SUCCESS GIRL 167
>
> **The Bold DIVA** 169
>> Quick Look 170
>> Who's That Girl? 170
>> The Elephant In Your Business 173
>> Inspirations for THE DIVA 177
>> Wake Up Your Inner DIVA 178

15 ~ Rock On With The Four Feminine Success Secrets 179

Conclusion 185

Afterword 187

Charts
> The 4 Biz Types and the 8 Feminine Types 48
> Core Motivations of the 4 Biz Types 50
> Strengths and Challenges of the 4 Biz Types 66
> My Feminine Type Profile 68
> The Feminine Type Success System Chart 73
> Business Strengths of the 4 Biz Types 87

*I'm a woman
Phenomenally.
Phenomenal woman,
That's me.*

~Maya Angelou

Introduction

This book puts a bright spotlight on you! You will discover the leading lady role you play in your life and business—your Feminine Type. You will uncover your hidden beliefs about money, power, business and success that may be limiting, or even sabotaging you. Step-by-step you will discover your own unique signature of feminine power by understanding:

- ✓ Your Feminine Type
- ✓ Your Superpowers
- ✓ Your Biz Type(s)
- ✓ Your Highest Business Potential
- ✓ Your Feminine Type shadow
- ✓ Your Biz Type shadow

Imagine how your business could change if you truly embodied your feminine power! The possibilities are endless. Yet, it is not always easy to see our greatness or to let others see our greatness. Women are experts at hiding—shrinking themselves down to please other people or focusing on their flaws. This book will help you recognize and own your unique feminine power instead of hiding it away.

With my Feminine Type Success System, I have guided hundreds of women to understand the impact of their Feminine Type on their business. You will find their stories throughout this book. They demonstrate the power of gaining self-awareness and then making a few strategic changes.

They have:

- Transformed their relationship with money and made more money.
- Transformed their relationship with themselves and found work they were truly passionate about.
- Transformed their relationship with power and stepped into their power.
- Transformed their relationship with sales and made more sales.

Join me on this adventure of self-discovery and self-mastery. If your business is already doing well, you will gain powerful insights to skyrocket your success and happiness. If you are struggling in your business, you will uncover the possible reasons along with the secrets to get your groove back.

The truth is the sky is the limit, so there is no point in limiting yourself. The Feminine Type Success System will help you put your crown on and rock your business like a queen! You will reclaim all the parts of yourself so you can create the business you want and the success you deserve.

If you are a life, business or career coach, you can use The Feminine Type Success System as both a resource guide and an assessment tool for your clients. It can streamline your understanding of their strengths and challenges—providing a powerful container for their empowerment and future growth. Understanding Feminine Types is also very useful for branding and marketing coaches.

Just take a step forward with me and follow the yellow brick road to discover **your Feminine Type**.

Joy Balma

1

Who Put This Elephant In My Business?

Nothing ever goes away until it teaches us what we need to know.
~Pema Chodron

Being a business owner is not for the faint of heart. You are the master architect of your business—you create all your results. It can be hard to take responsibility for what you have created, especially when you are not getting the results that you want. Under these circumstances, it's easy to feel like a victim.

Sometimes, despite all of our best efforts, we can come to a standstill in our business—as if there is an elephant sitting right in our way. We try pushing her, but she won't budge. We try ignoring her, but then she gets even bigger. We try every trick in the book, but she has a mind of her own.

It is natural to hope that our big ole elephant will move, if we just change everyone and everything outside of us. We want to think that our limitations are due to our circumstances or to other people. But when we make those external changes, alas, our loyal elephant follows us there too. We can't shake her. Everywhere we go, there she is—our elephant! Eventually, we learn to walk around her and just try to ignore that she is there.

If you are like me, you have probably wished for a magic wand that could make your elephant disappear with just one flick of your wrist. What I discovered was that we can make our elephant disappear, but the magic we seek comes from looking within and making changes. It takes real courage and honesty to do this—the willingness to go through a transformation. The only way to create real change is to change ourselves.

*The only way to create real change
is to change ourselves.*

There is something wholly unique about having your own business, because it brings up all your stuff. If you are stubborn, then stubborn is going to be written across the sky for you. If you can't keep your boundaries, then a sign will hang above your head flashing it in neon lights. If you are unwilling to change, then you might want to duck because a 2 X 4 is coming your way. It is up to you to read the signs and make changes. No one can do this for you.

When you have your own business you are playing a very big game. It is different than being employed—you have to take responsibility for what you create and then quickly adapt, change and grow. There isn't a moment to waste. Problems in your business mount when you:

- Can't see your patterns
- Don't take responsibility for your patterns
- Are unwilling to change, adapt and grow

Ignoring your patterns seems harmless, but what happens is this:

- When you can't see your patterns, you *complain*.
- When you see your patterns but don't take responsibility for them, you *blame*.
- When you are not willing to change, adapt and grow, the results of this become very apparent in your business—you're stuck! And then you start to feel *shame*.

This pile up of *complain, blame and shame* turns you into a victim —and keeps you there. We all know this person. As soon as you start talking to them, they launch into their victim story. They want you to agree with them—that they are indeed the victim of the other people or the circumstances in their life. When you listen to them tell their story, it is easy to see how invested they are being a victim. Yet, it is hard to see ourselves doing this same thing.

If you find *you* are circulating the energy of *complain, blame or shame*, use it as a cue to look inward. These are energetic traps that only serve to keep you stuck. They hinder your growth, your prosperity and your success. You can't go anywhere new when you are invested in complaining, blaming or shaming—because it deflects all responsibility away from you. If you play the victim, your underlying assumption is that you are powerless and worthless and it is someone else's fault.

> *If you play the victim,*
> *your underlying assumption is that you are powerless*
> *and worthless and it is someone else's fault.*

So sure, the elephant in your business makes you feel stuck, but it is actually a sign that it is time to start working your business from the inside out—and that means growing. You might as well welcome your elephant. It's much better than becoming that victim. Go ahead and paint your elephant pink with polka dots and put her in a tutu if you like—have a little fun with her! She is actually here with a very important message and she will vanish into thin air when her purpose has been fulfilled.

2

Follow The Yellow Brick Road

*"You've always had the power Dorothy.
You just had to learn it for yourself."*
~ Glinda The Good Witch, *The Wizard of Oz*

Our patterns play out in slow motion. It isn't until we see their cumulative effects in our business, that they become readily apparent! Even when our patterns become apparent, we often don't know what to do about them. We just go back to being ourselves and then our patterns repeat—otherwise known as self-sabotage.

This is why understanding your Feminine Type is so incredibly useful. It pinpoints your patterns and helps you take responsibility for the results you are getting. Understanding the feminine archetypes that are running your life is like having a powerful light that can guide you out of the darkness.

> *Understanding the feminine archetypes that are running your life is like having a powerful light that can guide you out of the darkness.*

I have always had my own business, so I know all about this journey—both the joys and the challenges. After a career as an interior designer, I went back to school to earn two Masters degrees in psychology and Chinese medicine. I then founded a Women's Wellness Center, where I worked as an acupuncturist and life coach with a specialty in personality typing. While all this sounds great, the truth is I had experienced many dark nights of the soul trying to understand my own patterns that kept showing up in my business—particularly the one of under earning.

My unravelling came when I turned forty—I had just ended a ten year relationship and I was sitting in a Laundromat. At this time, I was renting a room in a friend's house, because that was all I could afford. So there I sat with my two Masters degrees, a basket full of laundry and my broken dreams. I was supposed to be a success by now.

A little voice in my head reminded me, at regular intervals, that I was a colossal failure! It would say, "How is it possible that you could be this educated, yet broke and now alone?" Struggling financially became my little pet shame, and feeling like a failure cast a shadow on everything I did.

Sitting in that Laundromat, alone and broke was not the scenario I had set out to create for myself. My mind was spinning as to how I got here. There are those pivotal times in life when everything unravels. The good news is that crisis is filled with opportunity. Sometimes we have to go all the way to the bottom, before we are willing to make profound changes.

I was convinced that I had made a wrong turn somewhere, which landed me in this Laundromat beating myself up. I knew that if I didn't discover how I got here, I would repeat my pattern.

I recognized that the same patterns that were in my business had shown up in my relationship. I struggled with the balance between taking care of myself and taking care of others—*a classic female dilemma*. In both my business and my relationship I was over-giving, leaving money out of the equation and not wanting to disappoint people. I was also trying to solve everyone's unhappiness and I was not creating clear boundaries.

I believed I had done everything right—*really* right! I already knew about personality typing. I had studied it in graduate school and even wrote my final thesis on this subject. And yet, it didn't seem to be helping me to see my patterns—and this was even more frustrating!

It was clear to me that there were pieces missing to this puzzle ... pieces I needed to discover.

That day in the Laundromat I was so frustrated, confused and disappointed that I made it my mission to uncover the changes that I needed to make. I gathered up my basketful of disappointments, my last drop of courage and set out on an adventure to uncover what was beneath the patterns in my business. Like Dorothy in *The Wizard of Oz*, I put my foot on the yellow brick road hoping it would take me all the way home.

*The good news is that
crisis is filled with opportunity.*

3

The Good Girl's Handbook

As soon as you hang your shingle out to start your business, the person who shows up at your door is you! You create your reality, so what shows up in your business are your hidden beliefs—in the form of people and experiences. It takes a lot of courage to take responsibility for what shows up in your business, but once you do your business will begin shift. It all starts with working your business from the inside out. In my case, what was showing up was the Good Girl syndrome.

It seems I had ripped a page right out of The Good Girl's Handbook and unknowingly made it my business manifesto. The page read …

> *"Good Girls keep their desires small,*
> *put their needs aside—seeking only to give, and never get."*

The truth is, I could have written this Handbook. I couldn't believe that I had buried my ambitions under the guise of being selfless. Reading further along in *The Good Girl's Handbook* …

> *"Good Girls don't focus on money.*
> *Good Girls shrink their needs down so they aren't needy or greedy.*
> *Most of all, Good Girls are not selfish!"*

It took me a long time to uncover my hidden beliefs. One of them was that focusing on money meant I was selfish. No wonder I struggled with money. No wonder I had a strong reaction when I saw other women focusing on money in their business. My highest value was selflessness, so I judged people if they pursued money. They infuriated me in fact. My strong reaction was a clear sign that I had a shadow.

My hidden scripts and my shadow were running my business and they were running me into a ditch! With this insight I had to reevaluate all my ideas about money, power and what it meant to be a woman in business. I needed to examine how I was unconsciously giving my power away.

Your hidden beliefs and your shadow run your business. There is nothing more valuable or empowering than uncovering them.

It became clear to me that women have their own unique psychology around money, business, power and success that is very different from men. I felt that there needed to be an assessment system specifically for women. This would have to be a system that would help them claim all the different parts of themselves: their power, their patterns and their shadow.

With my background in personality typing and psychology, I went to work. I drew from everything I already knew about personality typing: the Five Elements from Chinese Medicine, Myers-Briggs, the Enneagram and Jungian Psychology/Typology. But because I was focusing on women's issues, there were missing pieces to this puzzle. I had to look closely at feminine power.

It took me a long time to put the missing puzzle pieces together. When I did, I created The Feminine Type Success System. It is unique in that it illuminates a woman's strengths and challenges—like a GPS for the feminine soul.

It was through my creation of The Feminine Type Success System that I finally recognized my own Feminine Type as THE SEEKER/

SAINT. This means that if I am not careful, I can get caught up in the potential imbalances of this type which consists of over-giving and leaving money out of the equation. My system also showed me that my shadow type was "The Leader." This means I can unknowingly reject money, power and success. That's right—leave money on the table and walk away.

My journey of self-exploration took me to a whole new level of personal power and prosperity, but first I had to uncover these hidden patterns. This book will guide you to uncover your own unique Feminine Type and your shadow type too. It will shine a bright light on both your strengths and your challenges—so you can bank on your strengths and bust through your blind spots, moving you into greater business success.

The Feminine Type Success System
illuminates a woman's strengths and challenges—
like a GPS for the feminine soul.

4

What's Success Got To Do With It?

When you know yourself you are empowered.
When you accept yourself you are invincible.
~Tina Lifford

Being a woman entrepreneur is a great opportunity for self-discovery and self-mastery, if we pay close attention. We are ultimately here to grow and evolve, so our business can be an extraordinary playing field for the evolution of our consciousness—if we let it.

Whether we are successful or struggling, our business continually pushes us out of our comfort zone showing us precisely where we need to grow. It challenges us to make the changes necessary in order to survive and thrive. Anything that needs to be healed or revealed is going to come up—you can count on it.

Our business can be an extraordinary playing field for the evolution of our consciousness, if we let it.

The first step on the path of owning your feminine power and transforming your business is to become aware of your definition of success—so it isn't rendering you powerless—*and even sometimes hopeless*. There is no point in nurturing an idea of success that is neither true nor useful.

We have all been handed down our ideas of success from society. We are told to focus on the bottom line—money. It all comes down to concrete ideas about winning or losing, success or failure, profit or loss. It is easy to get our self-worth seriously tied up in knots over these very narrow definitions of success—I know I did.

Your business success doesn't actually have the power to validate your worth. It never has and it never will—only you have the power to validate yourself. In fact, this is your responsibility. You are empowered to the extent that you know this. So, if your ideas of success are holding you hostage, let them go.

Success happens on many subtle levels that cannot be measured by bank accounts and bottom lines. Success is in the million tiny steps that you take toward your goals—it is in how you grow and in what you learn along your business path. When you do this, you're wearing the ruby slippers and you have all the power. Eventually you realize the truth that no one can limit you except you.

Wise women know that success is more like a spiral—a circular path of exploration—that is as much about self-discovery as it is about arriving at a perfect place called success. Success, like life, is a process and we are all works in progress.

When Oprah Winfrey walked onto her first television show, she wasn't the Oprah she is now. She evolved and grew over many years and she was proud of this. This was one of the reasons that she became so popular and famous. She showed people that success isn't about perfection. It's about continual transformation. We all watched Oprah struggle as she turned her challenges into wisdom, empowerment and a vast financial empire.

Success is not a static destination point. It is about being willing to grow and learn from your challenges. You don't have to be perfect now or ever! You just have to be willing to grow as you go.

Redefine success for yourself, so that it doesn't reduce you down to a sound bite of success or failure. There is only one failure, and that is the failure to love, accept and validate yourself all along your business journey. Ironically, when you get to that illusive place called success, you will have the same curriculum—to love, accept and validate yourself.

5

Your Girl Power

Above all, be the heroine of your own life, not the victim.
~Nora Ephron

The second step on the path of owning your unique feminine power and transforming your business is to recognize that you are a powerful creator and this is your birthright. Call it your girl power, your superpower or your feminine genius—you have it and it's time to claim it!

There is nothing more important for your business success than to realize that you are worthy and powerful. The media gives women a constant barrage of reasons to feel inadequate. If you buy into this, self-doubt can be tied to you like a ball and chain. Just like Cinderella had to believe in herself to get to the ball, you must do the same. Don't let self-doubt steal your magic—all it will succeed in doing is limiting your success, your money and your dreams.

As a business owner, *you* are the greatest asset you have! You definitely want to be able to use *all* your power—so you can rock it. This book is a step-by-step guide to help you do just that. You will discover that there are many kinds of feminine power—not just the ones that have been marketed to us by the media.

Understanding your Feminine Type is Business Savvy 101, because it helps you own your unique kind of feminine power. It gives you a ticket to ride your elephant—complete with a bird's-eye view of the changes you need to make and the direction you want to take.

Take a look at the following list. Notice if there is one feminine archetype that resonates with you the most. Although you have many roles that you play, see if you can pick just one. Which one sounds like you the majority of the time?

The Loyal SWEETHEART
The Nurturing SAINT
The Responsible EXCELLENCE GIRL
The Knowledgeable GODDESS GEEK
The Creative MUSE
The Free-Spirited SEEKER
The Ambitious SUCCESS GIRL
The Bold DIVA

I think my Feminine Type is:

It may be easy to find the one Feminine Type that resonates with you right away or it may be hard to pick just one. Actually, you are a combination of all of them. They are powerful archetypal energies. Some play a smaller role and others play a much larger role in your life.

Each of the eight Feminine Types represents essential qualities within us all. A wise woman accesses all these parts of herself, because she knows they all have power and wisdom. There is no one Feminine Type that is better or worse than another, and there is no one Feminine Type that trumps another. They all have strengths and challenges in equal measure.

You may feel a resistance to identifying yourself as one single Feminine Type, because you don't want to be trapped in a role you think you have to play. This book supports you in your freedom. Identifying your Feminine Type won't box you in. It will let you out of the box you're already in. Your Feminine Type is the role in which you feel most comfortable. It is your home base, but you will grow from there.

*Identifying your Feminine Type won't box you in.
It will let you out of the box you're already in.*

Think of yourself as the leading lady of your life. You play yourself in this role, and you've been playing her for as long as you can remember. In fact, she was well established by the time you were in grade school, and she is probably running your business right now!

It is important that you know all about this leading lady role of yours. If you don't—the role plays you. This means that you live out her script on autopilot—asleep, and this is how you end up repeating patterns that don't actually work for you. But don't worry, once you identify your Feminine Type you can regain control of your destiny.

So put your foot on the yellow brick road, and let's go on this journey—where you will claim and accept all the different parts of yourself, even the parts you may have hidden away. Along this road, you will uncover your unconscious beliefs about money, success and power. With the awareness you gain, you will be able to start a domino effect of positive change in your business and life. If I can do it, so can you!

The Feminine Type
~ Questionnaire ~

In the following questionnaire, there are no right or wrong answers—just the answer that is true for you. As you answer the questions, assign points to each statement based on how much the statement sounds like your usual way of being or thinking—the way you have been your whole life.

You may be tempted to answer the questions in terms of how you would like to be, but resist this temptation. You are always evolving and growing, but you have a core personality pattern that you need to identify in order for The Feminine Type Success System to assist you in the most powerful way.

- **YES THAT'S ME!- 3 points**
- **SOMETIMES THAT'S ME- 1 point**
- **NO THAT'S NOT ME- 0 points**

Assign each statement the appropriate point value depending on how much the statement sounds like you.

____ I tell people what they want to hear so I can avoid any conflict.

____ I want to be nice, so I have been known to overcommit and then I can't keep all those commitments.

____ I lack clarity around my goals. It's easier to help others with their goals.

____ People always relax around me. I put people at ease.

____ I dislike being negative or pushy, so I avoid any uncomfortable conversation.

___ I feel responsible when others aren't happy, and I try to help them.

___ I am very easy going, sometimes too easy going. I often don't speak up.

___ It is challenging for me to create boundaries with people.

___ It's very hard for me to ask my clients for money. I avoid money matters.

___ I have a lot of trouble saying no when I need to, and yes when I want to.

___ **Total Group 1**

___ People see me as warm and nurturing. I mother people.

___ I have often rescued people financially, and then I feel unappreciated for it.

___ I don't enjoy work if I am not personally helping people one-on-one.

___ I have a hard time creating boundaries with clients or colleagues.

___ I follow my heart and not my wallet, so I don't pay attention to my money like I should.

___ I am an over-giver, but I just can't help myself. I like to be generous.

___ I am empathic and intuitive. I am keenly aware of other people's feelings.

___ I love to give help, and I'm not as comfortable receiving help.

___ I don't want to look like I am bragging or self-centered, so I don't promote my business like I should.

____ I don't feel people appreciate what I give them, and I often am resentful about this.

____ **Total Group 2**

____ Responsibility, integrity and my principles are my main motivators and values.

____ It is very important to me that things are done right. I feel accomplished and proud of myself when they are.

____ Even though I don't want to be this way, I can punish myself for making small mistakes.

____ I love to fix things when I see inefficiency.

____ My life revolves around order, efficiency and boundaries.

____ I'm a big planner. Organization is very important to me.

____ I can interpret feedback from others as having made a mistake.

____ I obsess over details. I can't relax until I make things perfect.

____ I need certainty in my life. Predictability is very important to me.

____ I set impossibly high standards for myself—and I never feel I can reach them.

____ **Total Group 3**

____ I excel at work that involves structure, logic and reason.

____ I take information that is extremely complex and make it simple for others.

___ I carefully analyze every detail before I buy anything, and then I still might not make a purchase.

___ I like safety, certainty and reliability. I don't take big risks.

___ I like to look good, but my fashion style is practical.

___ I am an intellectual and analytical person.

___ I'm more interested in books and learning than in fashion and socializing.

___ I pride myself in being logical and levelheaded and not driven by my emotions.

___ I am recognized as having expertise in my field.

___ My idea of fun involves books, data, history and research.

___ **Total Group 4**

___ My passion in life revolves around creative self-expression and the arts.

___ I wish I could just do my art and leave money out of it. Money is so boring.

___ I am a rebel and an original. I dislike the thought of being like everyone else.

___ I have a unique, out-of-the-box perspective on life. I always have.

___ My fashion is my priority in life. It is a way to express my individuality.

___ I am more sensitive than everyone else.

___ I am known for my creativity, innovation and imagination.

___ Being unique is extremely important to me.

____ I need a lot of downtime to process my feelings, do my art and reflect.

____ I have a flair for the dramatic, and I love fantasy.

____ Total Group 5

____ I don't like rules or structure. I love to go with the flow.

____ I like change, variety, options and the unknown. Surprise me!

____ I am often overwhelmed and scattered trying to accomplish my business goals.

____ I miss out on things because I won't commit to them.

____ I find it impossible to do work that I don't have a passion for.

____ I'm always looking for my next adventure. I live to explore.

____ I've uprooted myself many times in my life to follow my bliss.

____ I choose my freedom over financial security in my life.

____ I don't need the approval or validation of others. I do my own thing.

____ I create my life so I am free to explore! I can't be boxed in.

____ Total Group 6

____ I am popular and social. I have a lot of friends and connections.

____ Being the center of attention is a big part of who I am.

____ I am driven to succeed and achieve and my personal life has been known to suffer.

____ I will push my budget over the brink to buy "the best."

____ I'm a Type A girl. I have a long to-do list. I am always on the go multitasking.

____ I have always had a very strong drive to succeed. I am very ambitious.

____ I am very positive and confident. I expect success.

____ I am competitive. I want to be number one. I hate to lose or come in second.

____ My fashion style includes designer labels, accessories and expensive bling.

____ My achieving can take over my life and exclude my relationships.

____ **Total Group 7**

____ I am the boss. I can't have people telling me what to do.

____ I am known for my bold "in your face" attitude and voice.

____ I am interested in having power. I don't like weakness. I won't show weakness.

____ I communicate in a direct and straight forward way, and this can intimidate people. I just tell it like it is.

____ I pursue power, money and influence.

____ I don't like people questioning my authority. It bothers me.

____ I have always had a very strong sense of my personal power.

____ I can be intimidating, combative and confrontational.

____ I like to talk, and people have told me that I don't always listen.

____ Take me or leave me. I'm not changing.

____ **Total Group 8**

Tally your scores

Maximum possible score is 30 and lowest possible score is 0 per group.

Group 1 __11__ The Loyal SWEETHEART

Group 2 __17__ The Nurturing SAINT

Group 3 __12__ The Responsible EXCELLENCE GIRL

Group 4 __18__ The Knowledgeable GODDESS GEEK

Group 5 __20__ The Creative MUSE

Group 6 __9__ The Free-Spirited SEEKER

Group 7 __14__ The Ambitious SUCCESS GIRL

Group 8 __12__ The Bold DIVA

Your Feminine Type is actually a combination of your top two scores which blends two archetypes together—such as THE SAINT/ SEEKER or THE SUCCESS GIRL/ GODDESS GEEK or THE MUSE/ DIVA etc. Your top two scores make up your Feminine Type.

My Feminine Type is:

SAINT / SWEETHEART

Example: THE MUSE/ SWEETHEART

Now that you know your Feminine Type, perhaps you are tempted to flip the pages ahead and read about yourself. Go ahead, but we have just begun our journey. If you read ahead, be sure to return here. There is so much more to learn so you can rock your Feminine Type and rock your business.

6

You've Got Superpowers!

*The most common way people give up their power
is by thinking they don't have any.*
~Alice Walker

With your Feminine Type in hand now, the next thing you want to know is that you've got Superpowers! Your Superpowers are special qualities that come so naturally to you that you might not think of them as Superpowers. They are deceptively simple, but don't underestimate them. Your Superpowers are your magic and your magnetism, and you definitely want to rock your magic! Your Superpowers are what draw people to you.

The Superpowers of the Feminine Types

- THE SWEETHEART'S Superpowers—*acceptance and kindness*
- THE SAINT'S Superpowers—*intuition and compassion*
- THE EXCELLENCE GIRL'S Superpowers—*high standards and flawless execution*
- THE GODDESS GEEK'S Superpowers—*knowledge and expertise*
- THE MUSE'S Superpowers—*style and originality*
- THE SEEKER'S Superpowers—*passion and open-mindedness*
- THE SUCCESS GIRL'S Superpowers—*confidence and ambition*
- THE DIVA'S Superpowers—*courage and charisma*

Since your Feminine Type is a combination of two types, this means that you have two sets of Superpowers. Write down your Feminine Type in the following box and then add your Superpowers.

My Feminine Type is:

SAINT / SWEETHEART

Example: THE DIVA/ SAINT

My Superpowers are:

INTUITION & COMPASSION — ACCEPTANCE & KINDNESS

Example: Courage & Charisma - Intuition & Compassion

Now, think even bigger for a moment. Your Superpowers represent a very special quality in you—a light that you radiate. When people see your light, it has the potential to awaken in them the highest qualities of your Feminine Type. This is because we have all the Feminine Types within us. For example:

- THE SWEETHEART shines the light of acceptance. She awakens THE SWEETHEART in others, the part of them that accepts others as they are.

- THE SAINT shines a light of compassion. She awakens THE SAINT in others, the part of them that knows each person matters and we are all in this together.

- THE EXCELLENCE GIRL shines the light of excellence. She awakens THE EXCELLENCE GIRL in others, the part of them that wants to be their best and to do their very best.

- THE GODDESS GEEK shines the light of knowledge. She awakens THE GODDESS GEEK in others, the part of them that recognizes the gift, responsibility and the privilege of our mind.

- THE SEEKER shines the light of passion. She awakens THE SEEKER in others, the part of them that is passionate about the exciting adventure called life.

- THE MUSE shines the light of individuality. She awakens THE MUSE in others, the part of them that knows their presence is unique on the planet and what they offer humanity is one of a kind.

- THE SUCCESS GIRL shines the light of confidence. She awakens THE SUCCESS GIRL in others, the part of them that knows they are a powerful creator—worthy of all that they want to create.

- THE DIVA shines the light of courage. She awakens THE DIVA in others, the part of them that knows how to stand strong in the face of obstacles in order to manifest her goals.

Your Superpowers are not only your own gift, but also a gift that you give to others. Part of accessing your feminine genius is to understand your Superpowers. They are your magic and your magnetism—what attracts people to you.

7

Every Queen Rules Her World

Think like a queen, a queen is not afraid to fail.
Failure is just another stepping stone to greatness.
~ Oprah Winfrey

The next step on your yellow brick road is to put your tiara on, because you rule your world—your business world that is!

Along with your Feminine Type, you also have your own particular Business Type, or Biz Type. Your Biz Type represents an area of your business where you have extraordinary skills. When you understand your Biz Type, you can rule your business world like a queen.

There are 4 Biz Types:
The Nurturer - The Expert - The Creative - The Leader

- THE SAINT and THE SWEETHEART are The Nurturer Biz Types. They excel in the relationship area of their business.

- THE EXCELLENCE GIRL and THE GODDESS GEEK are The Expert Biz Types. They excel in the knowledge area of their business.

- THE MUSE and THE SEEKER are The Creative Biz Types. They excel in the creative area of their business.

- THE SUCCESS GIRL and THE DIVA are The Leader Biz Types. They excel in the leadership area of their business.

With your Feminine Type in mind, look at the following chart to discover your Biz Type(s). You will notice right away that you may have two Biz Types, or one, depending on your Feminine Type.

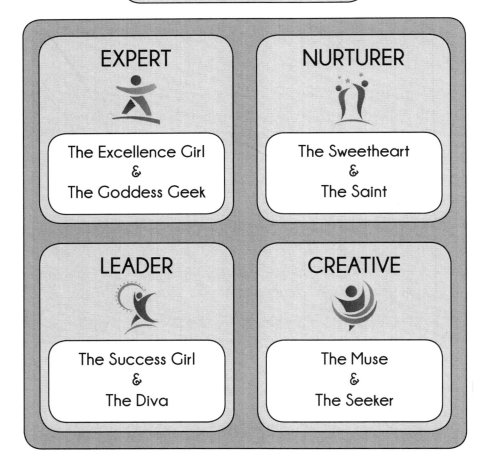

For example, if your Feminine Type is
THE SWEETHEART/ EXCELLENCE GIRL,
you are a Nurturer-Expert Biz Type.

If your Feminine Type is THE SWEETHEART/ SAINT,
your Biz Type is The Double Nurturer.

Fill in the box below with your Feminine Type and your Biz Type(s).

> ## My Feminine Type is:
>
> *NURTURER*
>
> Example: THE SWEETHEART/ EXCELLENCE GIRL
>
> ## My Biz Type(s) are:
>
> *DOUBLE NURTURER*
>
> Example: The Nurturer - Expert

The 4 Biz Types

It is easy to understand the Biz Types by looking at their core motivations—the driving forces in their life.

- **The Nurturer Biz Types** are motivated by *service, connection, belonging, and relationships*.

- **The Expert Biz Types** are motivated by *excellence, efficiency, structure and knowledge*.

- **The Creative Biz Types** are motivated by *freedom, individuality, exploration and self-expression*.

- **The Leader Biz Types** are motivated by *money, influence, status and achievement*.

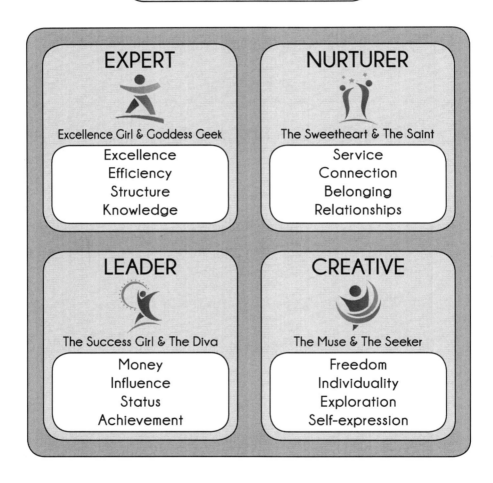

Your Biz Type(s) show you where you have your strengths, but along with your strengths come challenges. The great news is that by knowing your strengths and your challenges, you have a key to transform your business. So, let's look closely at the Four Biz Types.

THE NURTURER
Biz Types

The Saint & The Sweetheart

"I am nurturing. Clients like and trust me."

THE SAINT and THE SWEETHEART are The Nurturer Biz Types—they excel in the relationship area of their business. Their core motivation is service, connection, belonging, and relationships. They want to help people.

Strengths

THE SWEETHEART and THE SAINT can have a powerful healing presence. Encouraging and supportive, they listen to people in a way that makes them feel seen and heard. Clients easily like and trust them.

They thrive in businesses where they are able to help, support and care for people one-on-one. As you can imagine, Nurturer Biz Types are often drawn to the helping professions.

They are also gifted at building communities and organizations, because they excel at working collaboratively. They can be excellent networkers, because they enjoy people and easily make new connections.

Challenges

Pleasers, givers and accommodators, THE SWEETHEART and THE SAINT have a hard time saying no when they need to. They want to be generous and selfless, so they can get into trouble by over-giving. They avoid creating boundaries with people and this creates problems in their business: they lower their prices, don't charge enough and can often even give their services away. These imbalances reflect the fact that The Nurturers often don't focus on money or on their own needs.

Being givers, they can struggle with receiving. The Nurturers put themselves at the bottom of the list, and then never get around to taking care of themselves. In this way, they block their flow of receiving. All their energy goes outward in an attempt to give.

With their tendency to attend to the needs of others, they can abandon their own dreams. Slowly, self-doubt creeps in and they forget they are worthy and powerful creators—they abdicate their thrown and their journey is to reclaim it.

If your Feminine Type is THE SWEETHEART/ SAINT, you are a double Nurturer Biz Type. This means that both the strengths and challenges of this Biz Type are doubled in intensity for you.

THE EXPERT
Biz Types

The Goddess Geek & The Excellence Girl

"My work is high quality. Clients know I am competent and capable."

THE GODDESS GEEK and THE EXCELLENCE GIRL are The Expert Biz Types—they excel in the knowledge area of business. Their core motivation is excellence, efficiency, structure and knowledge. They want to produce quality work that they can be proud of.

Strengths

THE EXCELLENCE GIRL and THE GODDESS GEEK are the logical, linear thinkers of the Feminine Types. They are hard workers who demand excellence from themselves. Clients see them as knowledgeable, competent and capable.

The Expert Biz Types dislike seeing anything work improperly and their minds are always on the hunt for something they can fix or improve. They love to perfect, analyze, design, organize and refine. THE EXCELLENCE GIRL and THE GODDESS GEEK have the knowledge and skill to accomplish whatever they set their mind on. They are task oriented.

Challenges

The Experts are motivated to produce their highest standard of work and to be recognized for it. Yet, as hard as they work to perfect themselves and their work, they can still feel as though they are not good enough or don't know enough.

They have no trouble meeting their deadlines for others. More than likely, they will deliver ahead of schedule and surpass their client's expectations. However, when they work on their own projects, their attachment to being seen as excellent can leave them in a perpetual state of preparation and procrastination. If they can't do something perfectly, they probably won't do it. They avoid situations where they don't shine.

Intelligent and capable, The Experts like things done the right way and they can be uncompromising about it. This is both their greatest strength and their greatest challenge. They can be so demanding on themselves that they hold themselves back in their business.

The Expert Biz Types are on a journey to find the perfection in imperfection by letting go of control and going with the flow.

If your Feminine Type is THE EXCELLENCE GIRL/ GODDESS GEEK, you are a double Expert Biz Type. This means that both the strengths and the challenges of this Biz Type are doubled in intensity for you.

THE CREATIVE
Biz Types

The Muse & The Seeker

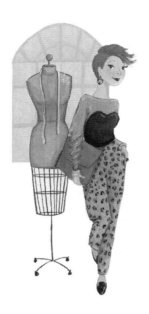 

"I am passionate. Clients feel inspired and intrigued by me."

THE MUSE and THE SEEKER are The Creative Biz Types—they excel in the creative area of business. Their core motivation is freedom, exploration and self-expression. They want to express their individuality.

Strengths

Fiercely independent, The Creative Biz Types march to the beat of their own drum. They inspire, transport and transform others with their innovative perspectives and insights. Clients find them inspiring and are intrigued by them.

Freedom of expression is the core of their identity. The Creative Biz Types always try to do work they have a real passion for. They need to follow their bliss.

Challenges

The Creative Biz Types never have a shortage of brilliant ideas. In fact, they have so many ideas they are easily overwhelmed and then they can become unproductive. Completing their creative projects is their challenge.

Independent by nature, they avoid anything that might impede their freedom, their expression and their expansion—even money. Like the classic starving artist or spiritual seeker, they may decide it's better to be unattached to money in order to remain free. Over time, this may mean that they struggle to create a solid financial foundation.

Being rebels at heart, The Creatives are independent. They have to be sure that they don't take this too far and isolate themselves.

If your Feminine Type is THE SEEKER/ MUSE, you are a double Creative Biz Type. This means that both the strengths and challenges of this Biz Type are doubled in intensity for you.

THE LEADER
Biz Types

The Diva & The Success Girl

"I am influential and confident. Clients recognize me as a leader."

THE DIVA and THE SUCCESS GIRL are The Leader Biz Types—they excel in the leadership area of business. Their core motivation is to gain power, status, influence and money. Ambitious by nature, they are driven to be successful.

Strengths

They have an indomitable spirit and natural self-confidence which makes them fearless in going after what they want. They are willing to take big risks, so they can win big. The Leader Biz Types are extroverts who know how to push through obstacles to reach their goals. They go for their big dreams and won't settle for anything less. Being ambitious, they are driven to accomplish, achieve and succeed. They know how to socialize, make powerful connections, promote themselves and build influence.

The Leader Biz Types feel confident they can make money, and they don't apologize for making it a priority in their lives. They are continually expanding their business and clients see them as confident leaders.

Challenges

The Leader Biz Types see life through a competitive lens. THE DIVA can have an I-am-the-boss attitude, and THE SUCCESS GIRL can have an I-am-the-star mindset. They have to be careful they don't take this too far because it can create power struggles in their relationships.

The Leader Biz Types move forcefully in the direction they want to go. It is important that they find the balance point between being cooperative and being competitive. They can leave their relationships in the dust in the pursuit of their dreams if they are not paying attention.

If your Feminine Type is THE DIVA/SUCCESS GIRL, you are a double Leader Biz Type. This means that both the strengths and challenges of this Biz Type are doubled in intensity for you.

Strengths & Challenges of the 4 Biz Types

EXPERT
Excellence Girl & Goddess Geek

Responsible & Capable; they produce quality work.

Challenged with perfectionism and over analysis; over-controlling.

NURTURER
The Sweetheart & The Saint

Encouraging & Nurturing; they are likable.

Challenged with money, over-giving, & not creating boundaries.

LEADER
The Success Girl & The Diva

Dynamic & Driven; they are powerful manifestors.

Challenged with relationships due to competitiveness and power struggles.

CREATIVE
The Muse & The Seeker

Passionate & Creative; they are innovators.

Challenged with money, being scattered and feeling like they don't fit in.

You may wonder whether a woman who is a Nurturer Biz Type can be a leader, or if a woman who is a Leader Biz Type can be creative? The answer is a resounding yes! You are never limited by your Biz Type. We have all these sides to us. The benefit of understanding your Biz Type(s) is to know where most of your energy and attention goes throughout the day and the dynamics/patterns it can create. With this information, you will know precisely how to bank on your strengths and bust through your blind spots.

Your Strengths can turn into your Weaknesses

Most people play to their strengths. This is natural because it is their comfort zone. The problem with this is that when you rely too heavily on your strengths—they can turn into your weaknesses. It is like Cinderella's carriage turning back into a pumpkin at midnight—you've stayed at the ball just a little too long. But don't worry! Your journey through The Feminine Type Success System will show you exactly how to avoid this.

Putting it all Together

Congratulations! You are starting to recognize your unique signature of feminine power in your business.

- ✓ Your Feminine Type—your unique girl power
- ✓ Your Superpowers—your magic and magnetism
- ✓ Your Biz Type(s)—the business world you rule.

You now have a much bigger picture of yourself as a businesswoman. Gather up all that you have learned and create your Feminine Type Profile.

~ My Feminine Type Profile ~

My Feminine Type is:

SWEETHEART / SAINT

Example: THE SAINT/ SEEKER

My Superpowers are:

Example: Intuition & Compassion - Passion & Open-mindedness

My Biz Type(s) are:

Example: The Nurturer-Creative

Service ★
connections
belonging
relationships

8

The Feminine Type Success System

Step into your Highest Potential

You may be wondering where you are going with all this. The answer is to the top! Every woman has her own individual style of success and business potential—because every woman is different.

- THE SWEETHEART becomes The Successful Collaborator
- THE SAINT becomes The Successful Humanitarian Entrepreneur
- THE EXCELLENCE GIRL becomes The Passionate Visionary
- THE GODDESS GEEK becomes The Inspired Wisdompreneur
- THE MUSE becomes The Empowered Creative
- THE SEEKER becomes The Trailblazing Goddess
- THE SUCCESS GIRL becomes The Inspirationista
- THE DIVA becomes The Global Transformer

For example, if you are a MUSE/ SWEETHEART, your highest business potential is to be The Empowered Creative- Successful Collaborator. Write down your highest business potential according to your Feminine Type.

My Feminine Type

SAINT / SWEETHEART

Example: THE MUSE/ SWEETHEART

My Highest Business Potential is:

SUCCESSFUL HUMANITARIAN / SUCCESSFUL COLLABORATOR

Example: The Empowered Creative - Successful Collaborator

Now it's time to create your Feminine Type Success System Chart so you can start the process of fulfilling your highest business potential.

- Turn back to Chapter 5 where you completed the Feminine Type questionnaire.
- Transfer all your scores from the Feminine Type questionnaire into The Feminine Type Success System Chart.
    - **Put a star by the <u>one</u> individual Type** that got your HIGHEST score on the questionnaire.
    - **Put an X by the <u>one</u> individual Type** that got your LOWEST score on the questionnaire.
- **TOTAL your scores for each of The Four Biz Type Quadrants:** Nurturer, Expert, Creative and Leader.
    - Put a plus sign by your **HIGHEST** scoring Biz Type Quadrant.
    - Put a minus sign by your **LOWEST** scoring Biz Type Quadrant.

The Feminine Type Success System™ Chart

EXPERT
 —

Excellence Girl 13
Goddess Geek 8

Total 21

NURTURER
 +

The Sweetheart 19
The Saint 23 ~~A~~

Total 42

LEADER
 —

The Success Girl 14
✗ The Diva 7

Total 21

CREATIVE

The Muse 16
The Seeker 18

Total 34

Now that you have filled in The Feminine Type Success System Chart, let's put it to work. The Chart adds a whole new layer of valuable information because you can see the totals for each Biz Type Quadrant. This helps you drill down even further to understand your power, your patterns and your shadow.

Start by bringing your attention to your lowest scores:

- You put an X by your lowest scoring individual Type. **This is your Feminine Type shadow.**

- You put a minus sign by your lowest scoring Biz Type Quadrant. **This is your Biz Type shadow.**

There is tremendous significance to your lowest scores because they represent your shadow. You want to be able to own both your light and your shadow because this is when you have the most power. You have already discovered your light in your Superpowers and in the strengths of your Biz Type. Now it's time to discover your shadow because it will help you rock your Feminine Type to rock your business.

9

Turn Your Shadow into Your Light

When sleeping women wake, mountains move.
~Chinese Proverb

Your Feminine Type Shadow

The next step on your yellow brick road is to awaken your sleeping giant within—your shadow. Your shadow consists of the personality qualities that you are not currently accessing, but that can move you toward greater business success if you did.

Think of your shadow as a place where you have unclaimed gifts. Your shadow can empower you. By befriending it, you can transform yourself and step into your highest business potential. This is the power of The Feminine Type Success System—it shows you where your shadow is. You have two shadows: your Feminine Type shadow and your Biz Type shadow.

Let's start with your Feminine Type shadow. Look at The Feminine Type Success System Chart. Find the one Type you marked with an X and write it down in the box below. This represents the individual Type you scored the lowest on in the Feminine Type questionnaire.

> **My Feminine Type Shadow is:**
>
> THE DIVA
>
> Example: THE SEEKER

There is great wisdom to be gained from your Feminine Type shadow. The truth is, she is a part of you that can empower you. For a quick look at what that wisdom is, go to the end of her individual chapter where you will find a section called "Wake Up your Inner..." There you will get a sneak peak at some of her best qualities—qualities you want to awaken in yourself.

The Sweetheart with a Diva shadow

Imagine, for example, that your highest scoring individual Type is THE SWEETHEART and your lowest scoring individual Type is THE DIVA. This means THE DIVA is your Feminine Type shadow.

Believe it or not, THE DIVA is a part of you too. You may feel a resistance to this Feminine Type. There is a natural tendency to resist your shadow, but it is important to know that your Feminine Type shadow has some qualities you could really use in your business. The strengths of your shadow propel you toward success. They represent power you are not using. Remember if you rely solely on your strengths, they can turn into your weaknesses no matter which Feminine Type you are. By stretching yourself out of your comfort zone and into your shadow, you will move into your highest business potential.

For example, as THE SWEETHEART, you may decide that you want to adopt some of THE DIVA'S courage to push through obstacles so that you can reach your goals. This means that courage is a quality you are not accessing as much as you could. You don't have to adopt courage in the same way THE DIVA does. You can adopt courage in your own way. When you borrow qualities from another Type, you don't become that Type, you merely enhance your own Type.

For example, you could use courage to help you speak up, step up and show up more boldly in your business. You could use courage to help you move in a whole new direction in your business. It is just a matter of giving yourself permission to own this quality for yourself.

The strengths of your shadow propel you toward success

At some point, you will want to read the entire chapter on your Feminine Type shadow, so you can learn how to access all of her power for yourself. After you do, come back and answer the following questions:

- What does she know that I want to know?
- What does she do that I would like to do?
- What power and wisdom does she have that I want to have?

_____

_____

_____

Your Biz Type Shadow

Now let's look at your Biz Type shadow. Your Biz Type shadow is another place where you have unclaimed gifts that are essential for your business success. Your Biz Type shadow contains your dormant power—you want to wake it up and put it to work for you.

You can find your Biz Type shadow by using The Feminine Type Success System Chart. Here's how:

1. Looking at the Feminine Type Success System Chart, find the Biz Type Quadrant where you have your **highest overall score**. (You put a plus sign by it.)

My Highest Scoring Biz Type Quadrant is:

NURTURER

Example: The Nurturer Biz Type

2. Find the Biz Type Quadrant where you have your **lowest overall score**. (You put a minus sign by it on The Feminine Type Success System Chart.)

My Lowest Scoring Biz Type Quadrant is:

EXPERT/LEADER

Example: The Creative Biz Type

This is your Biz Type Shadow

3. In the following groupings, find one group that matches your highest and lowest scoring Biz Type Quadrants. The title of each grouping hints at the benefits you will receive when you borrow from the strengths from your Biz Type shadow.

Highest score: THE CREATIVE BIZ TYPE
Lowest score: THE LEADER BIZ TYPE

Up Your Game

You are very creative and innovative, but you can expand even more by waking up your inner Leader. It's time to get business oriented about your ingenious ideas. The Leaders can inspire you to bring your creativity and money together. They can help you "up your game."

Read the individual chapters on THE SUCCESS GIRL and THE DIVA. Claim their best qualities for yourself. How could they help you reach your goals?

_____

_____

Highest score: THE CREATIVE BIZ TYPE
Lowest score: THE EXPERT BIZ TYPE

Create a Foundation for your Dreams

As a Creative, you have many brilliant ideas but you could use some help in bringing your ideas to fruition or else they just sit on your drawing board. The Experts know how to organize, plan and deliver results. Borrow their best qualities for yourself to bring structure to all your brilliant ideas.

Read the individual chapters on THE EXCELLENCE GIRL and THE GODDESS GEEK. Decide what qualities they have that you want for yourself. How could they help you reach your goals?

_____

_____

Highest score: THE CREATIVE BIZ TYPE
Lowest score: THE NURTURER BIZ TYPE

Grow Your Tribe

As a creative rebel, you love your journey, but it can also be lonely on the road less traveled. Pay a visit to The Nurturers. They possess the missing piece to your puzzle and are happy to share it. Pick up some of their secrets to growing your tribe and expanding your community.

Read the individual chapters on THE SWEETHEART and THE SAINT. Decide which of their best qualities you want for yourself. How could they help you reach your goals?

_____

_____

Highest score: THE EXPERT BIZ TYPE
Lowest score: THE CREATIVE BIZ TYPE

Follow Your Bliss

You are an Expert Biz Type, but ask yourself if in working so hard you may have lost your spark? It is important to keep your creative juices flowing. The Creatives can help you find your purpose, passion and inspiration. Add their best qualities to your bag of tricks, so you can get inspired to follow your bliss.

Read the individual chapters on THE MUSE and THE SEEKER and turn them into your allies in success. Decide which of their best qualities you want for yourself. How could they help you reach your goals?

_____

_____

Turn Your Shadow Into Your Light

Highest score: THE EXPERT BIZ TYPE
Lowest score: THE LEADER BIZ TYPE

Take Center Stage

You work hard by attending to all the details. You are an expert in your field, but nothing happens in your business if you don't promote yourself. Spend some time reading about The Leader Biz Types. They can show you how to stretch out of your comfort zone and kick your dreams up a notch. There is a whole new world waiting for you when you take center stage.

Read the individual chapters on THE SUCCESS GIRL and THE DIVA. What qualities do they have that you would like to adopt? How could their best qualities help you reach your goals?

_____

_____

Highest score: THE EXPERT BIZ TYPE
Lowest score: THE NURTURER BIZ TYPE

Pave your Road to Success

You are disciplined. You know how to keep your nose to the grindstone. But notice if you forget the importance of making connections, relationships and partnerships—oh my! You want all of these on your road to success. Follow the yellow brick road over to The Nurturers. They can help you discover new ways to relate, communicate and connect. Borrow their wisdom and you will pave your road to success.

Read the individual chapters on THE SWEETHEART and THE SAINT. Decide which of their best qualities could help you become more empowered in your business. How could they help you reach your goals?

_____

_____

> Highest score: **THE NURTURER BIZ TYPE**
> Lowest score: **THE CREATIVE BIZ TYPE**

Add Kicks to your Mix

You're friendly and easygoing, but are you blending in too much? If so, it's time to break away from the crowd so you can be seen and heard. Find out what is unique about you and then highlight it. Take a cool, hip trip over to The Creatives camp and add some of their kicks to your mix.

Read the individual chapters on THE MUSE and THE SEEKER. What qualities do they have that you would like to adopt? How could their best qualities help you reach your goals?

_____

_____

> Highest score: **THE NURTURER BIZ TYPE**
> Lowest score: **THE LEADER BIZ TYPE**

Get Your Moxie On!

Consider the advantages of reading The Rebel's Guide to Success! Just think, you can help a lot more people if you soak up the strengths of the Leader Biz Types. Just a drop of their supercharged moxie can inspire you to show up and speak up like never before. Get your moxie on!

Read the individual chapters on THE SUCCESS GIRL and THE DIVA. What qualities do they have that you would like to adopt? How could their best qualities help you reach your goals?

_____

_____

Highest score: THE NURTURER BIZ TYPE
Lowest score: THE EXPERT BIZ TYPE

Clear a Path

You put all your energy into helping people. This is your comfort zone, but notice if you have left organization, structure and boundaries behind. Without them, things can get messy. Look in on The Experts. Notice the advantage they have in running a tight ship! Borrow their magic wand to clear a path to your business success.

Read the individual chapters on THE EXCELLENCE GIRL and THE GODDESS GEEK. Claim their best qualities for yourself. How could they help you reach your goals?

_____

_____

Highest score: THE LEADER BIZ TYPE
Lowest score: THE NURTURER BIZ TYPE

Reconnect

As a Leader Biz Type, you are always expanding your business empire—this is your nature. But in order to expand even more, you want to borrow the qualities of The Nurturers. They can inspire you to powerfully connect with people in a way that increases your influence, success and happiness.

Read the individual chapters on THE SWEETHEART and THE SAINT. Turn them into your allies. How could adopting some of their qualities help you reach your goals?

_____

_____

Highest score: THE LEADER BIZ TYPE
Lowest score: THE CREATIVE BIZ TYPE

Passion Pays

As a leader, it is vital to lead with passion. Passion has power. What is really driving you to succeed? What is your inspiration? The Creatives can remind you to stay connected to your passion and your authentic self. When you discover what truly moves and inspires you, you will shine even brighter.

Read the individual chapters on THE MUSE and THE SEEKER. Claim their best qualities for yourself. How could they help you reach your goals?

_____

_____

Highest score: THE LEADER BIZ TYPE
Lowest score: THE EXPERT BIZ TYPE

Don't Forget the Details Diva

You're a leader who loves to achieve and succeed, but don't forget the details diva. The Experts can help you polish up your act. Borrow their best qualities for yourself. They can show you how to up level your expertise so you can expand your influence and status even more.

Read the individual chapters on THE EXCELLENCE GIRL and THE GODDESS GEEK. Claim their best qualities for yourself. How could they help you reach your goals?

_____

_____

Business Strengths
OF THE 4 BIZ TYPES

EXPERT

Excellence Girl & Goddess Geek

Organization
Structure
Quality
Expertise

NURTURER

The Sweetheart & The Saint

Relationships
Community
Connection
Communication

LEADER

The Success Girl & The Diva

Focus on Money
Ambition
Promotion
Visibility

CREATIVE

The Muse & The Seeker

Passion
Inspiration
Innovation
Individuality

Identifying your Biz Type shadow is essential for business transformation. Without this awareness, we can remain stuck in our old patterns indefinitely. For example:

- If you have a Leader shadow, you may be separating yourself from money.
- If you have a Nurturer shadow, you may not be connecting with people.
- If you have a Creative shadow, you may be disconnected from your passion and purpose.
- If you have an Expert shadow, you may be circumventing all the details and work you need to do to reach a level of mastery in your field.

Harnessing the power of your shadow is about welcoming an essential quality into your life that you have been unconsciously rejecting. If you have been unconsciously rejecting something, it needs to be welcomed and integrated in order for you to reach your highest potential in your business.

All you have to do is move toward the best qualities of your Biz Type shadow just a little more every day. As you adopt the best qualities of your Biz Type shadow, you can feel enthused and excited about what you can create in your business—it opens the door to new opportunities. Think of your Biz Type shadow as the missing link in your business. Make a list of the highest qualities of your Biz Type shadow. Let them become your qualities too.

~ AMANDA ~
Feminine Type: THE EXCELLENCE GIRL/ SAINT
Biz Type: The Expert-Nurturer

Amanda was an EXCELLENCE GIRL/ SAINT. This meant she was an Expert-Nurturer Biz Type. Her Biz Type shadow was The Leader. Even though she was a top level executive, she told me she was having trouble owning her authority. She was caught up in pleasing people and trying to be perfect. She worried what people would think of her. She had been dreaming of a vacation to Italy for years, but never took it. She couldn't even leave work early for fear of what people might think of her, and yet she was the boss. She was not owning her power and rightful authority.

As Amanda understood more about her Feminine Type, she felt released from the duty of playing out its script on autopilot. She wanted to expand beyond the confines of pleasing and perfecting. I gave her a simple suggestion to write on a piece of paper, "I am the boss. I can do what I want and it is okay if people see me as the boss." She took my suggestion and looked at the piece of paper throughout the day. This reminded her to get off her autopilot of pleasing and perfecting, so she could own the privileges of being the boss.

A year later my client had taken that trip to Italy, had frequently left work early and was no longer feeling like she had to shrink herself to please others. She also made massive changes in every area of her life where she wasn't owning her full authority and power. She started jogging and lost weight, and she let go of employees that weren't up to par.

Amanda had been unwilling to own her power and authority. She was afraid it might displease someone if she did. The Feminine Type Success System helped her pinpoint her Biz Type shadow, so she could claim her power. When she did, the floodgates opened and she made swift progress. She went to work transforming every area of her business that she had been unwilling to before.

10

The Eight Feminine Types

Congratulations! You have been on an amazing journey to discover your unique feminine power and magnetism. You have uncovered:

- ✓ Your Feminine Type
- ✓ Your Superpowers
- ✓ Your Biz Type(s)
- ✓ Your Highest Business Potential
- ✓ Your Feminine Type shadow
- ✓ Your Biz Type shadow

Now it's time to look at the eight individual Feminine Types. In the following pages, you will get a backstage pass into their world. As you read about each one, appreciate them as part of yourself and learn from them. We have all of these archetypes within us. They each have their own unique charm and their own unique challenges.

Remember that your Feminine Type is a combination of your top two scoring Types. For example, a woman whose Feminine Type is THE EXCELLENCE GIRL/ DIVA is a totally different Feminine Type than a woman who is THE EXCELLENCE GIRL/ SWEETHEART.

- THE EXCELLENCE GIRL/ DIVA will be a highly ambitious and driven woman with uncompromising standards of excellence.
- THE EXCELLENCE GIRL/ SWEETHEART wants to please people perfectly.

This second Feminine Type is much more accommodating than the first. So, keep in mind that you are a *blend* of your top two scoring types.

To help you with this, write down your Feminine Type below. Then, as you are reading, make notes on their primary characteristics and qualities so you can blend the two types together.

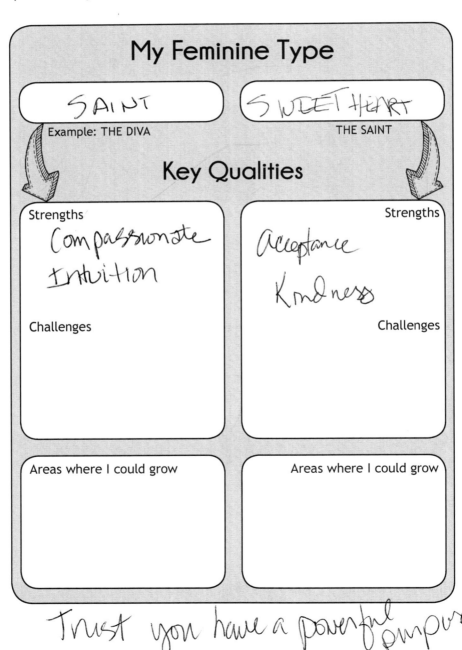

My Feminine Type

Left box: SAINT (Example: THE DIVA)

Strengths: Compassionate, Intuition

Challenges:

Areas where I could grow:

Right box: SWEETHEART (THE SAINT)

Strengths: Acceptance, Kindness

Challenges:

Areas where I could grow:

Trust you have a powerful purpose

11
The Nurturer Biz Types

The Loyal SWEETHEART
&
The Nurturing SAINT

The Loyal SWEETHEART

Quick Look

QUALITIES: Friendly, easygoing, shy, kind, loyal, supportive, trustworthy, reliable

BIZ TYPE: The Nurturer

BUSINESS POTENTIAL: The Successful Collaborator

SUPERPOWERS: Acceptance and kindness

FASHION STYLE: Soft fabrics, pastel colors, subtle patterns and delicate jewelry

COMMUNICATION STYLE: Friendly and easy going

DISLIKES: Conflict or negativity; being pushy or being pushed

MOTIVATION: Connection and belonging

OUT OF BALANCE: The Pushover

Who's that Girl?

No act of kindness, no matter how small, is ever wasted. ~Aesop

The Loyal SWEETHEART is the reigning queen of nice, but she doesn't wear a fancy crown or put on airs. She's really the girl next door—simple, humble and a little shy. She doesn't try to impress anyone or be someone she's not.

Her Superpowers are acceptance and kindness, which translates right into likability. She has a calm, nonjudgmental presence that allows people to relax and just be themselves. She patiently listens to people and they feel seen and heard by her. She has an astonishing ability to put her own needs aside and be there for the needs of others. She is a trusted friend and levelheaded advisor. Overtime, people often come to rely heavily on her. They need her. They trust her. She is the one person they know they can rely on—her reliability is a great gift she gives people. Because of this, THE SWEETHEART has tremendous influence on the people in her life—in her own quiet way.

In her business, people like and trust her too. She gets along with everyone and this is her lucky charm. She can walk into any networking group or event and easily make connections and friendships. She just needs to fine-tune a few things, so she can turn all her charm into gold.

> *She gets along with everyone and this is her lucky charm.*

THE SWEETHEART actually doesn't recognize the power of her innocent charm. She is humble. She tends to focus on others more than she focuses on herself, often shying away from the spotlight. THE SWEETHEART prefers to work from behind the scenes to support others in reaching their goals. She excels at providing essential support to other people.

She is the happiest when she is part of a community, where she can contribute and belong. She is the very fabric of any organization or business, doing whatever it takes to make them work. Being of service, creating harmony and building community are her strengths.

As a businesswoman, she knows the power of working collaboratively. She creates work environments that utilize everyone's talents. She is inclusive because she sees the best in people. THE SWEETHEART proves that you don't have to overpower people to be powerful. Acceptance and kindness have their own power.

THE SWEETHEART proves that you don't have to overpower people to be powerful. Acceptance and kindness have their own power.

Her highest business potential is to become The Successful Collaborator. Here, THE SWEETHEART harnesses her natural likability to create a community of loyal supporters. She is masterful at catalyzing people to work both with her and for her in fulfilling her vision. Once she owns her worth and power, there is no end to what she can create in her business. As a Successful Collaborator, she is like a powerful queen who rules with both strength and kindness.

The Elephant in your Business

When we're not trying to please other people, we begin to understand what's right for us. ~Byron Katie

Communicate or Stagnate

It is so natural for you to put your needs aside, it may not even seem like a problem to you—but it can become one. There is never anything wrong with being kind or nice—you just don't want to become a people pleaser and a pushover. If you do, it puts you in a precarious position in your business. You walk lightly and speak softly, avoiding any hint of conflict because you are trying to make everyone happy. If someone appears even slightly displeased, you go to work trying to accommodate them, and that can mean you:

- Lower your prices
- Overcommit
- Are unable to say no
- Leave money out of the equation
- Lack clarity and ambition

This also means you may give away your services and your time and not even notice it. Problems in your business can snowball when you decide that other people's unhappiness is your sole responsibility. You have to be careful not to lose your power, your voice and your money in an attempt to accommodate, please and make other people happy. The following story of my client Kendra shows how easy it is for the SWEETHEART to get caught up in the need to please others, only to end up frustrated.

~ KENDRA ~
Feminine Type: THE SWEETHEART/ EXCELLENCE GIRL
Biz Type: The Nurturer-Expert

Kendra's life was a fireball of frustration when she came to see me. She told me she wanted to quit her job as a nurse. I typed her as a SWEETHEART/ EXCELLENCE GIRL. Her Feminine Type shadow was THE DIVA.

Kendra wanted to please people perfectly. Co-workers were always asking her to take their shifts and work for them at different locations. Kendra would juggle her life around to accommodate their every request, yet these co-workers would not do the same for her. In fact, they were inconsiderate of her needs. Still, Kendra went to great lengths to accommodate them. She did it because she wanted to help people, but also because she wanted to be a nice person. She was attached to this idea of herself, so she was stuck accommodating everyone.

Kendra was trapped in the classic SWEETHEART pattern of being afraid to tell her truth, because she wanted to be nice. This meant she couldn't do what was right for herself and please others at the same time. As a result, everyone knew she was a pushover. By not speaking up, Kendra felt like an unappreciated victim. She was angry and frustrated all the time.

I suggested she practice saying no to requests made of her, even if she could easily accommodate them. Kendra had many instances to practice, because her colleagues were always trying to dump work on her. She had never told her colleagues no before and was surprised to see that they respected her when she did.

When she returned to our next coaching session, she told me that she was able to say no to requests made of her. It wasn't easy, but she was proud of herself and felt an emotional weight of frustration had been lifted from her. She recognized that her life had to work for her too.

Kendra couldn't continue her pattern of trying to be nice and then end up being unhappy and resentful. Through our coaching, she realized she loved her job and didn't want to quit. It was a perfect fit for her to serve people. She just needed to learn to tell her truth, and to know that she was still a nice person if she did.

The problem with hiding your true feelings is that eventually it creates misunderstandings and deep resentments that undermine your relationships. Relationships cannot survive if you don't tell the truth.

THE SWEETHEART is known for just leaving relationships and work situations in order to get away from people who don't seem to respect her boundaries. As you may imagine, this doesn't work. She can end up creating the same situation with the new people in her life. Leaving situations doesn't solve her real problem—which is that she doesn't communicate her real feelings or keep her boundaries. The good news is, once she does, she transforms her business and life.

Dream On

Your playing small does not serve the world. There is nothing enlightened about shrinking so that other people will not feel insecure around you. We are all meant to shine, as children do. ~ Marianne Williamson

When your people pleasing is out of control, you're imbalanced. Part of people pleasing includes not knowing what you want in your business—lacking clarity. Consider that your dreams for your business are your soul's navigation system. Your desires are seeds that reveal your purpose. It makes no sense to ignore them, but you are an expert at pushing your needs aside to be there for others. There are times when it is necessary to put your needs and desires aside, but not all the time, and not to the point of ignoring your own goals and dreams.

> *Your dreams for your business are your soul's navigation system. Your desires are seeds that reveal your purpose.*

The magic behind anything you want to create is to clearly identify what you want. This can be daunting, because feelings of fear can surface—fear that you aren't powerful enough to create what you want. Often not having clarity is a way to avoid experiencing these feelings. Yet, consider that it is impossible to create something that you haven't identified.

It may be new for you to focus on yourself. Take the time to get away from the demands of everyone in your life, so you can discover what your dreams and goals are for your own life. You will begin a whole new momentum in your business by clearly identifying what you want.

Inspirations for THE SWEETHEART

Everything that happens to you is a reflection of what you believe about yourself. We cannot outperform our own level of self-esteem. We cannot draw to ourselves more than we think we are worth. ~Iyanla Vanzant

The following inspirations can help you align with your highest business potential—The Successful Collaborator. The more you focus on creating these inner shifts, the more transformation and success you will see.

~ I create and keep boundaries with people.

~ I move toward my dreams and goals with clarity and passion.

~ I am paid well for my services.

~ I say yes to what I want.

~ I take my ambitions seriously.

~ I tell my truth to people even if it is difficult for them to hear.

~ I say no when I need to, and yes when I want to.

~ I know what I want. I ask for what I want.

~ I am a powerful creator.

~ I'm worthy of all the things I want to create.

~ I step up and speak up boldly.

Wake Up Your Inner SWEETHEART
~Connection and Belonging~

The end result of kindness is that it draws people to you.
~Anita Roddick

THE SWEETHEART knows that you rock your business when you create a sense of belonging with your clients, colleagues and community. If you scored low on THE SWEETHEART, you want to make her your partner in success. She has wisdom you need. Here is what you can learn from her:

- Accept people the way they are and they will accept you the way you are.

- Kindness has its own power. Don't underestimate it.

- You don't have to impress people—just be yourself.

- There is a time to let others have the spotlight and a time to take the spotlight.

- Be a good listener—it is the secret to connecting with people.

- Create community. People love to know they belong and are cared for.

- Ambition, money and kindness can all work together beautifully.
- Knowing how to create harmony is the asset you need for any kind of collaborative project.

The Nurturing SAINT

Quick Look

QUALITIES: Nurturing, helpful, friendly, service-oriented, empathic, intuitive

BIZ TYPE: The Nurturer

BUSINESS POTENTIAL: The Successful Humanitarian Entrepreneur

SUPERPOWERS: Intuition and compassion

FASHION STYLE: Comfortable, soft fabrics, pastel colors

COMMUNICATION STYLE: Encouraging, empathic

DISLIKES: Being selfish or self-centered; people who are selfish or self-centered

MOTIVATION: To be helpful, generous and selfless

OUT OF BALANCE: The Rescuer

Who's That Girl?

It is not how much we give but how much love we put into giving.
~Mother Teresa

The Nurturing SAINT is gifted at making people feel comfortable and, of course, nurtured. Her presence alone can be healing. She is the archetypal mother of the Feminine Types. It fills her heart with gladness to help those in need. Give her someone that needs her and she will gladly take them on as her newest project to love and heal.

If you are THE SAINT, you know it. You have taken people on as your projects your whole life. You often give what you don't have to give—and then you give some more. You look for places to help—places that need you.

No matter what business THE SAINT is in, she turns it into a mission to help people. In this way, she feels driven by a strong purpose. Like THE SWEETHEART, THE SAINT makes the happiness of others her top priority and even her responsibility.

> *No matter what business THE SAINT is in, she turns it into a mission to help people.*

THE SAINT'S Superpowers are her intuition and compassion. Her intuition makes her sensitive to the needs and feelings of others. She notices when people need help and she responds. She feels their pain and asks, "What's wrong and what can I do?" No gesture of help is too small: a smile to an overworked clerk, a compliment to a stranger who seems down, or helping someone to carry a bag.

THE SAINT is like a sponge. If she hasn't learned how to manage her intuition, she often can't tell the difference between her own feelings and the feelings of others. This can leave her feeling overwhelmed, confused and sometimes frustrated as to where to put her energy.

We all have compassion and intuition. THE SAINT is a part of us all, but the woman whose Feminine Type is THE SAINT is proactive in her giving. Helping others and being selfless is the core of her personality and she brings this right into her business.

As a businesswoman, THE SAINT effuses a friendliness and a warmth. She engages people by being genuinely interested in them and in wanting the best for them. Whatever her line of work, she finds a way to make it about service.

THE SAINT'S highest business potential is to be The Successful Humanitarian Entrepreneur. Here, she has learned to powerfully promote her business and make it profitable—allowing her to expand her humanitarian goals even more. She knows that it isn't selfish to ask for what she wants and to pursue her big dreams. Most importantly, she has mastered the balance between giving and receiving.

The Elephant in your Business

When we give cheerfully and receive gratefully everyone is blessed.
~ Maya Angelou

Learn to Receive

It is a lot of work to be a full time SAINT. You want to help everyone. Being generous is natural to you. You don't think twice about giving your time, energy or money wherever it is needed. Being overly generous seems harmless. It may even seem right to you. Actually this needs to be carefully monitored, because it can turn you into a rescuer which can start an avalanche of ineffectiveness such as:

- Failing to create contracts or boundaries
- Not calling people out on their bad behavior
- Doing other people's work for them
- Undercharging
- Rescuing people and drowning yourself

Close your eyes and imagine you are over-giving and over-delivering and never quite asking for fair compensation in return. Sure, you're a Saint, a broke Saint!

You know you are imbalanced when you aren't including money into your big picture and watching your bottom line. This is because focusing on money is secondary to your giving. It is vital for your business that you find your balance with giving and receiving. You don't want your virtues of selflessness and generosity to work against you. It can be hard to know exactly where to draw the line in your giving, but this is what you must learn.

~ LAURA ~
Feminine Type: THE SWEETHEART/ SAINT
Biz Type: The Double Nurturer

Laura came to me for coaching for her direct sales jewelry business. I typed her as a SWEETHEART/ SAINT which made her a double Nurturer Biz Type.

She told me she had decided that getting new representatives on her team would be the best course of action to build her business. In our coaching session, she described one situation after another in which she created no boundaries with her new representatives. She over-gave to them, which took up massive amounts of her time and energy.

For example, instead of spending two or three hours helping her new representative at her jewelry show, she would spend the entire day and do all the selling for them. Or she would go to lunch with a new rep prospect and spend four hours listening to them talk about their life story. Then, the prospect wouldn't be interested in signing up with Laura after all that time.

She explained that she felt desperate to have these new people on her team in order to reach her goals, so she was going overboard to accommodate them. The problem was that they were hesitant to work in the business in the first place. Laura hoped she could somehow mold them into a good sales force by stepping in and doing their work for them. I pointed out that she was modeling to them what they would be doing if they joined her business—exhausting themselves by over-giving.

Laura had been acting out of her long held, unconscious patterns that she needed to over-give and over-accommodate in order to feel valuable. We talked about the fact that it was impossible to motivate her sales reps by doing everything for them. I suggested she hold back her instinct to be overly generous and let her prospects meet her halfway, as this might attract people who were more eager and willing to work their own business.

Laura realized she was caught in a trap of trying to be selfless and rescuing others, but it was backfiring on her. Through our coaching, she started setting boundaries. Over time, she learned that she didn't need to over-give, rescue and over-accommodate people. She kept her boundaries and learned to say yes or no when it really worked for her, and the result was that people respected her. Laura also recognized that her over-giving meant she wasn't taking care of herself, and that made her feel resentful.

By keeping her boundaries with others, Laura took her jewelry business to a new level of success. She also made time for herself. In this process, she lost sixty pounds. Laura's experience demonstrates the transformative effect of understanding your Feminine Type, and the power of making just a few strategic changes.

When I last saw her, she had won a trip to Hawaii through her jewelry business, which was one of her original goals when she first came to see me. Laura never dreamed that she would lose sixty pounds, reach her business goal and regain her self-esteem all by understanding her Feminine Type.

As soon as you realize that you are over-giving, step back and find your balance. There is an element of self-betrayal in over-giving. Make sure that by solving the problems of others, you aren't ignoring your own.

It is only when you keep a balance between giving and receiving that your business will flourish. This internal shift can open up the floodgates of clients and money into your business and you have a chance to realize that giving and receiving are one in the same.

It is a scientific fact that your heart feeds itself first, before it sends blood through the rest of your body. Likewise, it is vital to the health of your business that you get the nourishment that you need.

> *There is an element of self-betrayal in over-giving. Make sure that by solving the problems of others, you aren't ignoring your own.*

Promote or Perish

For THE SAINT, a high priority is to avoid being selfish or self-centered. While this is a virtue you value highly, it can squelch your ability to promote your business services successfully. It can also take your focus off earning money. Promoting yourself feels like you are bragging, so you tend to avoid it. Putting money front and center in your business feels selfish. Yet, if you don't promote yourself, new potential clients can't find you and then you have no business. If you don't focus on earning money, you can't stay in business.

The truth is—being overly humble and selfless can end up being very costly. You may be an expert and even an authority in your field, but no one will know it if you don't tell anyone. Take a course or read a book on the art of tooting your own horn without feeling like you are bragging.

> *The truth is—being overly humble and selfless can end up being very costly.*

Promoting yourself includes building up your image and brand. Have professional photographs taken and put yourself out front and center in your marketing materials. Dare to stand out. Think of your business as a mirror of you. If you hide, your clients hide from you. Step into the highest version of yourself that you can imagine and put your marketing materials together to match that you! When you get this right, you'll be unstoppable.

> *Think of your business as a mirror of you. If you hide, your clients hide from you.*

Inspirations for THE SAINT

The following inspirations can help you align with your highest business potential—The Successful Humanitarian Entrepreneur. The more you focus on creating these inner shifts, the more transformation and success you will see.

~ I market and promote my business as powerfully as I can.

~ I let money serve me so that I can serve others.

~ I monitor my time carefully when I help others.

~ I trust my intuition.

~ I focus on making money in my business

~ I am as loyal to myself as I am to others.

~ I keep my eye on my bottom line.

~ I make self-care a priority in my life.

~ I clearly ask for what I want.

~ I create boundaries and make clear agreements with people.

~ I give generously and I receive generously.

Rock Your Feminine Type To Rock Your Business

Wake Up Your Inner SAINT

~Mission to Serve~

Nothing liberates our greatness like the desire to help, the desire to serve. ~ Marianne Williamson

THE SAINT knows that you rock your business when you have a mission to serve. What is your big why for doing your business? Who are you serving? Why is it important to you? How are you contributing to the betterment of humanity? THE SAINT knows that when you are connected to your mission of service, you are powerful. If you scored low on THE SAINT, she has wisdom you can use.

- Having a purpose bigger than yourself gives you passion and power.

- Helping your clients get what they want is how you succeed.

- Make your business a win-win for everyone and you will succeed even more.

- Your intuition is your greatest ally. Listen to it and use it.

- Be more forgiving than you think you should be. People are doing their best.

- Your ability to connect with people can determine your success.

- When you listen carefully to people, you build trust and rapport with them.

12
The Expert
Biz Types

The Responsible EXCELLENCE GIRL
&
The Knowledgeable GODDESS GEEK

The Responsible EXCELLENCE GIRL

Quick Look

QUALITIES: Thoughtful, dutiful, reliable, organized, productive, efficient, cautious, detail oriented and responsible

BIZ TYPE: The Expert

BUSINESS POTENTIAL: The Passionate Visionary

SUPERPOWERS: High standards and flawless execution

FASHION STLYE: Classic, traditional, practical, minimal jewelry

COMMUNICATION STYLE: The precise expert

DISLIKES: Inefficiency, being unproductive

MOTIVATION: Quality, excellence

OUT OF BALANCE: The Controller

Who's That Girl?

The Responsible EXCELLENCE GIRL leaps over the mundane matters of everyday life in search of her utopian ideals. She wants to refine herself and the world. Her attention to detail gives her eagle eyes to see what is inefficient, ineffective or unbalanced. She can also see what is exquisite, beautiful and balanced.

Her Superpowers are a combination of her high standards and flawless execution. Even on her worst day, she is excellent. Her impeccability elevates everything she does. She loves nothing better than a job well done and this makes work sacred for her. If she says she is going to do something, be prepared for her it to be done exceptionally well. She doesn't do anything halfway or halfheartedly. No detail is too small and she gives every task her all. She's the detail diva. THE EXCELLENCE GIRL tries to outsmart all the unknowns in a project by planning for every possible eventuality. While this can be exhausting, she can't relax until she has done her best and everything has been done to perfection.

*She doesn't do anything halfway or halfheartedly.
She's the detail diva.*

As an entrepreneur, THE EXCELLENCE GIRL prefers structure, safety and certainty—she wants to feel confident that she will do a good job and that she will make sufficient income. Dealing with the ups and downs that are part of being a business owner can be taxing on her. If her business struggles, she can take it personally and take it hard. It requires a leap of faith for her to trust the process. If she can make peace with the risks involved, she can put her visionary ideas into motion.

THE EXCELLENCE GIRL'S highest business potential is to be a Passionate Visionary. Here, she sees beyond her ideas of perfect or imperfect to the essence of things. She has learned to see the perfection in everything. She knows there is a magic can that happens when she let's go of control. When she is fueled with a powerful purpose, she is alive with passion.

The Elephant in your Business

Optimist: Someone who knows that taking a step backward after taking a step forward is not a disaster. It's the cha-cha. ~Robert Brault

Plan for Spontaneity

You have never been the kind of businesswoman who likes the theory of throwing spaghetti on the wall to see what sticks. That's just not your kind of business plan. You want everything to be planned and perfectly polished, so you can be your best at all times. But this may mean you miss the synchronicity and serendipity that can happen. While you produce excellent results with all your organizing, there are times when it is advantageous to drop all your plans and roll with what is happening. When you do, what happens is often much better than what you could have planned. There is a magic that happens when you let go of control and go with the flow.

~ AMY ~
Feminine Type: THE EXCELLENCE GIRL/ GODDESS GEEK
Biz Type: The Double Expert

Amy was in turmoil when she came to me for coaching. Her safe, but boring job was ending. At thirty years old, she had never had another job. It had been a reliable but joyless position. I typed her as THE EXCELLENCE GIRL/ GODDESS GEEK. This made her a double Expert Biz Type.

She explained that she had no idea what she wanted to do, but she knew for sure she didn't want to continue doing clerical work. She told me she wanted to feel passion for her work. Her Feminine Type shadow was THE SEEKER and she had a Creative Biz Type shadow. Amy needed to unlock the power of her shadow to both find and empower herself.

I suggested she start thinking about what would spark her interest, but the idea of even exploring her options was frightening to her. "What if I go down a wrong path?" she worried. I suggested she consider that there is no wrong path. She was not comforted by this idea. She hoped she could be smart enough to take the road that was certain to assure her success. Wanting to do the right thing is natural, but demanding certainties can be crippling.

Her only interest was yoga and she had taken a yoga teacher training course a few years ago. I asked her if she would like to take her interest in yoga further. Amy worried that she would not be able to make enough income from teaching yoga. She told me she wanted to love her work, but she also wanted financial success and security.

Amy's expectations were immobilizing her. She couldn't take a step forward, because it meant walking into the complete unknown. Unfortunately, you cannot bypass your journey of self-discovery. Universal Intelligence has a way of moving us along in our evolution, and it was Amy's time to grow beyond her safety net. I told her that this path of exploring her options might be uncomfortable at first. Yet, in order for her to find what she was looking for, she needed to let go and go with the flow.

After a time of resisting the idea of walking into the unknown, Amy started taking different classes to see what appealed to her. It was hard for her to be in this transition phase, between who she had been and who she was becoming. It challenged all her ideas of certainty, safety and what should be.

It took a year of being in this transition phase, before Amy realized she loved yoga and wanted to open her own yoga studio. Not long after, a perfect location opened up just walking distance from her home. She knew it was the right space at the right time for her. She admitted to me that even a month earlier she would not have been ready for this. She recognized that there was a divine timing in all of this that she couldn't have predicted or planned.

Amy learned to let go of her need to control outcomes, and in doing so she gave herself the time and space to discover the business that she truly loved. She surrendered to living in the flow as any good yoga teacher would suggest!

It is important for your own health and the health of your business, that you know when to let go of your ideas of the way things should be. There is only so much that you can micromanage. Sometimes the surprises of life are the most delightful. Call it coincidence, serendipity, synchronicity or the flow—be open to them and let them work for you. Plan for spontaneity.

It is important for your own health, and the health of your business, that you know when to let go of your ideas of the way things should be.

Stand Up to your Inner Critic

Perfectionism is the 20-ton shield we lug around thinking it will protect us when, in fact, it's the thing that's really preventing us from being seen and taking flight. ~Brene Brown

You've trained yourself to see flaws, and honed this skill over your lifetime. This means it can be hard to see anything else but flaws sometimes. You know this feeling, when your inner critic has all her engines revved and she's coming after you! She climbs right into your driver's seat and takes off in a blaze of glory. Your inner critic loves to tell you why you are not good enough to manifest your business goals, so it is vital to recognize when she has taken over. If you aren't questioning the stories she tells, you can easily believe them.

Her voice starts as a whisper telling you that you really shouldn't dream too big or hope for too much. Then it becomes a shout, saying that you're just not good enough to have what you want. It is vital to separate yourself from her stories. They are not the truth, and they never have been.

In *The Wizard of Oz*, Dorothy threw a simple bucket of water on the Wicked Witch of the West and this melted her. Likewise, your inner critic will melt as soon as you stand up to her. It may be hard to believe that you can defeat this inner adversary so easily, but the more you stand up to her, the smaller and weaker she gets.

> *Your inner critic will melt as soon as you stand up to her.*

You stand up to her by listening to her stories very carefully, until you can see that they are lies. Once you recognize her stories are not true, you reclaim your power—and then she can no longer take over your driver's seat.

The Wicked Witch of the West was threatening and frightening, but Dorothy conquered her and you can conquer your inner critic too.

Inspirations for THE EXCELLENCE GIRL

The following inspirations can help you align with your highest business potential—The Passionate Visionary. The more you focus on creating these inner shifts, the more transformation and success you will see.

~ I am enough now.

~ I stand up to my inner critic, and she backs down.

~ I know when to let go, and go with the flow.

~ I recognize the perfection in imperfection.

~I move toward my dreams and goals with
an open-minded curiosity.

~ I stop worrying about being perfect and just show up.

~I remain open to the magic in the moment.

~I choose to find the beauty in what is.

~ I allow for spontaneity and synchronicity and
let them work for me.

~ I relax my need to be right and perfect.

Wake Up Your Inner EXCELLENCE GIRL
~Devotion, discipline, dedication~

*The secret joy in work is contained in one word—excellence.
To know how to do something well is to enjoy it.* ~ Pearl S. Buck

THE EXCELLENCE GIRL knows that you rock your business when you follow through and complete your projects to the best of your ability. Discipline and focus make this happen. If you scored low on THE EXCELLENCE GIRL, you will want to learn her secrets.

- Complete your projects and enjoy the benefits of accomplishment.
- Your work is what you offer to the world. It is sacred.
- Your integrity matters. Be honorable and truthful in all your interactions.
- Do the absolute best that you can do.
- Go the extra mile—it pays off.
- Small acts of thoughtfulness and consideration for others go a long way.
- Discipline and dedication are the ways to accomplish any goal.
- Take the time to create work of true substance and high value.
- Create systems and structures that support you in working efficiently.
- Organization helps you succeed.

The Knowledgeable GODDESS GEEK

Quick Look

QUALITIES: Knowledgeable, logical, cautious, analytical, studious, intellectual

BIZ TYPE: The Expert

BUSINESS POTENTIAL: The Inspired Wisdompreneur

SUPERPOWERS: Knowledge and expertise

FASHION STYE: Practical, sensible. Minimal jewelry

COMMUNICATION STYLE: Facts, data, information and research

DISLIKES: Saying, "I don't know"

MOTIVATION: To be recognized for her knowledge and authority

OUT OF BALANCE: The Know-It-All

Who's That Girl?

Congratulations, you're a GODDESS GEEK! You're super smart! Everyone wants your skills. They can't live without you. You are intellectual, logical and analytical. While all women are intelligent in their own way, what sets THE GODDESS GEEK apart is her expertise. If you get her talking about her area of expertise, be prepared to listen for a long time as she downloads her volumes of knowledge—a telltale sign that you are talking to a GODDESS GEEK. Her knowledge base is stunning. She is a Google unto herself.

She is a Google unto herself.

THE GODDESS GEEK is authentically herself. She has her own quirky, yet practical fashion style that works for her. She doesn't feel the need to change herself to please anyone.

Curious about how everything works, THE GODDESS GEEK loves research, data, history, facts and learning. If she wants to speak a new language, she learns it. If she wants to play an instrument or sail a boat, she teaches herself. She is not daunted by a mental challenge—in fact, she thrives on it. She often is an expert on unusual and obscure subjects such as Egyptian hieroglyphics, maritime law or Russian poetry, for example. Her interests and expertise will surprise you.

THE GODDESS GEEK is an improvement and efficiency expert like her sister THE EXCELLENCE GIRL. They both hate to see anything working improperly and their minds are always on the hunt for new projects that beg for their meticulous attention to detail. They both bury themselves in their projects spending endless hours trying to perfect them. They are determined to contribute something exceptional with their time, energy and talents—doing mediocre work is not their style.

It is no surprise that THE GODDESS GEEK'S Superpowers are knowledge and expertise. She is an information junkie. She has the know-how that people need and this puts her in demand. Whatever she does, people clamor for her services, because she has the skills and information that improve their lives.

Whatever she does, people clamor for her services, because she has the skills and information that improve their lives.

As a businesswoman, THE GODDESS GEEK has the ability to express what is complex and makes it simple for others to understand—this is a great gift. For example, she could be a brilliant health professional who uses her expertise to resolve her client's difficult health challenges. She could be a book coach who navigates people through the complex maze of writing and publishing, or she could be a computer technology expert who assists her clients in the technical aspect of their business.

THE GODDESS GEEK'S highest business potential is to be The Inspired Wisdompreneur, but there is only one way to get there—to let go of everything she knows. When she does, she no longer cares about being the smartest person in the room or the one with all the answers. She can comfortably say, "I don't know." In doing so, she becomes truly wise. Her heart and mind are wide open and she is connected to her intuition. This ignites a great flow of energy, ideas, inspiration, creativity, people and money into her business.

The Elephant in your Business

Knowledge is learning something every day.
Wisdom is letting go of something every day. ~Zen proverb

True Wisdom

THE SWEETHEART has to be careful not to go overboard with her kindness because she can become a pushover. THE SAINT has to monitor her giving so she doesn't become a full-time rescuer. THE EXCELLENCE GIRL has to let go of control so she can find ease and flow. The GODDESS GEEK has to make sure that all her knowledge doesn't turn her into a know-it-all.

The problems is, you can't learn anything new if you already know it all. Ironically, the only way to have wisdom is to let go of everything you think you know. True Wisdom is found in being receptive—that means seeing everyone and every experience as an opportunity to grow. A receptive mind is simply the most expansive mind. A sure sign that you are imbalanced is if you are not receptive to the input, feedback, help and advice from others.

*Wisdom is found in being receptive—
this means seeing everyone and every
experience as an opportunity to learn and grow.*

When you become a know-it-all, it can put your business on a slippery slope in a number of areas of your business. One way is that you begin to imagine that you can do it all. This can play out in your business. For example, when you do your own website, branding, graphic design, marketing and promotion—you become a one-woman show. You hate hiring other people when you are able to figure it out yourself, yet you may want to consider doing so. The problem is you are not an expert in all of these fields. Just because you can do something doesn't necessarily mean you should. It is important to know when to call the experts in to help you.

~ HEATHER ~
Feminine Type: THE GODDESS GEEK/ SUCCESS GIRL
Biz Type: The Expert-Leader

Heather had her own natural cosmetics line and was a brilliant fountain of knowledge. She could speak for hours on the details of the ingredients she used and the process of how she created her natural cosmetics. She had a few high-end accounts, but she wanted to grow her business. She came to me for coaching, because she couldn't understand why she wasn't moving forward. I typed her as a GODDESS GEEK/ SUCCESS GIRL.

The problem was that she tried to be an expert at everything in her business. She had superb products, but her packaging, branding and website were not working well for her. She thought they were fine. I told her I could not navigate her website, but she didn't agree. She wrote the copy, built the website and did her own branding. She was attached to it and thought it was great.

I suggested she consider hiring someone to take over certain areas of her business: promotions, marketing, packaging and branding. The work she was doing in these areas was not matching the quality of her products. I recommended she let experts help take her to a new level, but Heather did receive this suggestion well. She thought she had done a good job, or at least a good enough job.

It took six months for Heather to decide to make changes and let the experts help her. She told me she asked a lot of other people about her website and branding and they told her the same thing I had. She eventually handed everything over to professionals and loved what they did.

Just because you can do something doesn't mean you should. There are aspects of business that every businesswoman needs to hand over to someone else. There is only so much time in a day. If you could let go of control, you would get more done, more efficiently and more effectively. As well, this can help you move into the things you do best.

Hook up your Intuition

One of the benefits of being a woman entrepreneur is being able to take full advantage of your intuition, but THE GODDESS GEEK often overrides it in favor of a rational argument. For example, someone approaches you with a business opportunity and it looks good on paper. However, you have this gut feeling that something doesn't feel right. Every time you think about this business opportunity you have this same feeling. Yet, you ignore it because it makes sense on paper.

Your intuition can be your inner voice, a hunch or a gut feeling. If you pay attention, you will discover the unique way your intuition communicates with you. It is a powerful resource that can benefit you in many important ways. Take some time to develop your relationship to your intuition, so it is there when you need it.

Develop your relationship to your intuition so it is there when you need it.

Inspirations for THE GODDESS GEEK

The following inspirations can help you align with your highest business potential—The Inspired Wisdompreneur. The more you focus on creating these inner shifts, the more transformation and success you will see.

~ I am open-minded.

~ I learn from others.

~ I listen to my intuition and use it.

~ I take inspired action in my business.

~ I make time for spontaneity, creativity and play.

eptive to the ideas, feedback and opinions of others.

etwork, expand my circle and create relationships that support my business.

~ I take time to find my balance in body, mind and spirit.

~I delegate to experts the areas that are not my specialty.

~ I can easily say "I don't know."

Wake Up Your Inner GODDESS GEEK

~Expertise and Knowledge~

THE GODDESS GEEK knows that you rock your business when you develop expertise and have extensive knowledge in your field. You may have many talents, but be sure to have expertise. This is what sets you apart from others in your field. If you scored low on THE GODDESS GEEK, you will want to wake her up.

- Expertise equals money—simple as that.
- Decide on your specialty as soon as you can.
- If you specialize, you differentiate yourself from your competition.
- You can charge more if you are an expert. If people pay too little, they don't see you for your expertise.
- Never stop learning.
- Develop mastery in your field.
- Having mastery in your field ensures you will be in demand.
- Stay curious.
- Learn from everyone.

13

The Creative Biz Types

The Creative MUSE
&
The Free-Spirited SEEKER

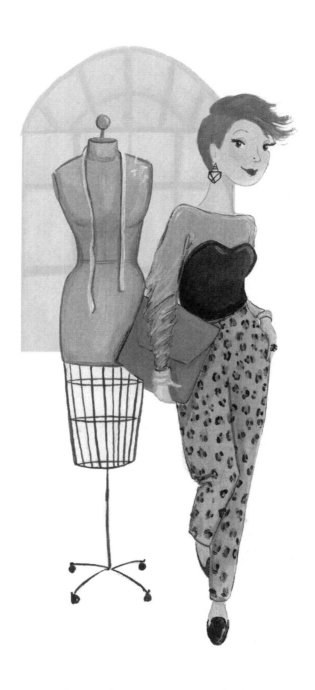

The Creative MUSE

Quick Look

QUALITIES: Creative, original, innovative, independent, rebellious, fashion oriented, artistic

BIZ TYPE: The Creative

BUSINESS POTENTIAL: The Empowered Creative

SUPERPOWERS: Style and originality

FASHION STYLE: Original & Trendsetting. One-of-a-kind jewelry and accessories

COMMUNICATION STYLE: Dramatic or hipster cool

DISLIKES: Being told what to do and how to do it

MOTIVATION: Self-expression and originality

OUT OF BALANCE: The Drama Queen

Who's That Girl?

In order to be irreplaceable one must always be different.
~Coco Channel

Pink hair one day, a new tattoo the next and then she tells you she is moving to France. THE MUSE can be a different person every time you see her. If everyone is going left, she goes right. If everyone wears plaid, she wears stripes. She likes being the purple zebra in the room.

THE MUSE is a fiercely independent rebel who thrives on being unique and doing life her own way. She hates the idea of being a cookie-cutter version of anyone else. She is a trendsetter and not a trend follower.

She ignites the imagination and curiosity of others by being mysterious and intriguing. She turns everything upside down to show you a different perspective! Expect the unexpected from THE MUSE.

THE MUSE is all about creativity and the arts, and she stimulates people to think in new ways. You can find her in all the artistic fields: music, design, writing, the culinary arts, dance, beauty, fashion, film, acting and performing. Even if she is not in the arts per se, everything she touches will get her personal flair. Her innovative mind can transform anything from drab to fab!

> *Her innovative mind can transform anything from drab to fab!*

Her Superpowers are her style and originality. THE MUSE expresses her individuality through art, fashion and design. She knows how to create an entire universe of intrigue with her singular style. Every MUSE has a love affair with her closet. Her wardrobe is one of the ways she defines and expresses her unique self.

THE MUSE loves having plenty of downtime to recharge and rejuvenate. She retreats into her inner cocoon to connect with her feelings and many moods. She enjoys spending time alone being self-reflective, journaling and, of course, creating her art. Being independent is a big part of who THE MUSE is. She just has to be careful that she doesn't isolate herself. It is vital for the health of her business that she stays in the loop, communicates and has a community to contribute her many talents.

As a businesswoman, THE MUSE brings a wealth of ideas, imagination and creativity into her business. Her ingenious creativity sparks the imagination and curiosity of others. She loves nothing more than being at the helm of her own creative empire. She is at her best when she is her own boss, otherwise she can't express herself fully.

THE MUSE has to do work that she feels connected to—because self-expression is the very fabric of her being.

Self-expression is the very fabric of her being.

Her highest business potential is to become The Empowered Creative. Here, THE MUSE engages, connects and contributes her artistic gifts. Her inventive perspectives transport, inspire and enrich others. Positive and focused on her goals, she knows money is a sacred exchange of energy and she welcomes it into her life. She is recognized for her creative genius and has a supportive community in her life.

The Elephant in your Business

*To be beautiful means to be yourself. You don't need
to be accepted by others. You need to accept yourself.*
-Thich Nhat Hahn

Be-you-tiful

Your strength is your authenticity, but finding and truly accepting your authentic self is a journey. You may have become a rebel as a way of separating yourself from others so you could find your authentic self. Sometimes this is necessary to sort through the ideas that everyone else has given you, or perhaps you need to sort through your own ideas about who you think you should be. Other people will always have their opinions about what is right for you, but nothing can replace your own self-authority. No one wants to be their authentic self more than the MUSE, but sometimes our authentic self is buried.

~ SONJA ~
Feminine Type: THE MUSE/ SWEETHEART
Biz Type: The Creative-Nurturer

Sonja was a fashion genius, but her parents wanted her to be in a more important and prestigious profession than fashion. And yet, she had this gift of styling people. She hid her talent for years. She took on more traditional jobs and studies to please her parents. Eventually, after she had a daughter, she recognized that something was missing in her career—herself.

In our coaching, she discovered she was a MUSE/ SWEETHEART Feminine Type. Sonja realized she was always afraid that her real self was not enough for her parents, so she wore a mask. She wanted her parents to accept her, so she did everything she imagined they wanted her to do—even denying her talent and authentic self. Being a SWEETHEART/ MUSE is a tricky combination. THE SWEETHEART part of her wanted to please her parents and this meant hiding her MUSE talents.

When Sonja understood her Feminine Type, it helped her see who she really was for the first time. Through our coaching, she changed careers and became a full-fledged fashion stylist. In her soul, this is who she had been all along. She just needed to accept herself and her true talents and passion.

Sonja made a decision to take off all her masks and be her full authentic self. In doing so, she was well on her way to her highest potential—The Empowered Creative-Successful Collaborator. She made swift progress in her stylist career. Once she both knew and accepted who she really was, she was no longer committed to pleasing other people at her own expense.

There is a very real magic that comes from honoring yourself and accepting yourself just as you are, but it isn't always easy if other people have expectations of you. Yet, accepting yourself illuminates your path, so that you can find the work that you are passionate about. This story shows the importance of understanding the two Types that make up your one Feminine Type.

Accepting yourself illuminates your path, so that you can find the work that you are passionate about.

Make Amends & Friends with Money

When the archetype of the starving artist is alive and well in the heart and mind of an artist, it can be daunting to make a living. THE MUSE may struggle to validate her own artistic gifts—not seeing them as worthy of making money. At the same time, she wants her work to be taken seriously. She wants to share her creativity and make money, but she worries she will be marginalized and become the starving artist. It is a conundrum.

The journey of THE MUSE mirrors that of all passioneers—a woman who combines what she loves to do with her business. The question is, "Can I make money doing what I love?" At some point, her answer has to be "Yes!"

Check to see if you have a limiting mindset around your art, creativity and making money. Ask yourself if you might have the following hidden money beliefs:

- Being creative and making money don't mix.
- Money interferes with my authenticity.
- You can either feed your soul or feed your wallet. You can't do both.

It is impossible to attract something that you are rejecting. Money is energy. There is no point in pushing it away. Embrace the flow of money, allow it into your life and envision having it. Think of money as another artistic expression of you. If you have a belief that says you can't make money as an artist, then you are stuck at go. There is always a way. It is up to you to open the door to the flow first.

It is impossible to attract something that you are rejecting. Money is energy. There is no point in pushing it away.

In order to become The Empowered Creative, it is vital that you don't become a victim of money. Put one foot in front of the other, and remember that you are a co-creator with the Universe. It is simply not productive to let yourself spin out into negative thinking and indulge in worst-case scenarios. It is important to keep your thoughts aligned with where you are going and what it is you want to create.

Remember that challenges appear in order to teach you something important, not to turn you into a victim. Pay attention to what you can learn. Let all your experiences, strengthen, enlighten and empower you. You just might discover that there is something good to harvest from every situation that will make you stronger, wiser and more successful.

Inspirations for THE MUSE

Don't you ever let a soul in the world tell you that you can't be exactly who you are. ~Lady Gaga

The following inspirations can help you align with your highest business potential—The Empowered Creative. The more you focus on creating these inner shifts, the more transformation and success you will see.

~ I let my authentic self shine brightly.

~ Money and creativity work together in my life.

~ I learn from my challenges and let them strengthen me.

~ I stay in the loop and stay connected to people.

~ I have a clear plan of action for my creative business.

~ Making money allows me to express who I am.

~ I validate and honor my artistic talents.

~ I am financially rewarded for my creative talents.

~ I am empowered with the help and assistance of others.

~ I welcome money into my life and let it work for me

~ I follow through on my business plan

Wake Up Your Inner MUSE
~Dare to be yourself~

If you are always trying to be normal, you will never know how amazing you can be. ~Maya Angelou

THE MUSE knows that you rock your business when you highlight your unique personality and style. You can learn from her how to stay true to your authentic self. If you scored low on THE MUSE, here is what you can learn from her:

- Stay true to yourself.
- Create a signature style and make it your statement.
- When you are inspired, you inspire others.
- Let your personality shine through—it helps people connect with you.
- Be yourself.
- Be willing to stand out.
- Celebrate your flaws. They are what makes you interesting.
- Get your creative juices flowing.
- The only way to innovate is to think outside the box.

The Free-Spirited SEEKER

Quick Look

QUALITIES: Independent, spontaneous, curious, insightful, enthusiastic, freedom-loving, innovative

BIZ TYPE: The Creative

BUSINESS POTENTIAL: The Trailblazing Goddess

SUPERPOWERS: Passion and open-mindedness

FASHION STYLE: Unstructured, ethnic patterns and jewelry

COMMUNICATION STYLE: Enthusiastic, positive, curious

DISLIKES: Limitations, boredom

MOTIVATION: Exploration, freedom, expansion

OUT OF BALANCE: The Scattered Dreamer

Who's That Girl?

All who wander are not lost. ~J.R.R. Tolkien

Certainties are boring for THE SEEKER. She wants to blaze a new trail. She is not satisfied living by the rule book of others. She wants to go beyond the known to explore the unknown. Life itself is the ultimate road trip and that means we are all adventurers and seekers—to some extent. The difference is that THE SEEKER is a passionate adventurer and born explorer—seeking is a way of life for her. She is, often, alternative in some way because she takes the road less travelled.

In the bestselling book and film, *Eat, Pray, Love*, Elizabeth Gilbert told her story about leaving the perfect suburban life, which felt like a trap to her. She didn't want to live a predictable life. She wanted to be free to grow and explore. Women around the world took refuge in her daring journey and travelled vicariously along with her on her adventure. Her story is an example of how a SEEKER has an irrepressible desire to explore.

If THE SEEKER chooses the traditional path of marrying and having a family, she'll continue to passionately grow, explore, seek and dream. Nothing will stop her, so it is important for the people in her life to understand her wanderlust.

> *It is important for the people in her life to understand her wanderlust.*

THE SEEKER'S Superpowers are her passion and open-mindedness. She is gifted at seeing possibilities everywhere. Innovative ideas and solutions flow from her. She is an asset in any brainstorming session. Endlessly curious, THE SEEKER has picked up a wealth of skills over the years and she is talented in many different fields. On any day, you will find her floating seamlessly between her many different interests—juggling them all.

If her questing turns inward, she can become a spiritual seeker. She could follow a particular religious tradition, but she is more likely to hop from one spiritual teacher (or tradition) to another like a hummingbird, sipping nectar from each flower. THE SEEKER isn't usually a joiner. She often prefers her independence, so she can continue exploring and expanding.

As a businesswoman, THE SEEKER finds a way to make her passion pay, and her work play. She can be the ultimate passioneer—a woman who combines what she is passionate about with her business. Any Feminine Type can be a passioneer, but this often means she has to carve out her own path.

~ JACKIE ~
Feminine Type: THE SEEKER/ SAINT
Biz Type: The Creative-Nurturer

Jackie's passion was travel and she was determined to build her life around it. She followed her bliss and started a Meetup group for travel enthusiasts. She launched a blog on travel and gathered a following. Committed to her passion, she attended blog conferences to learn how to build her community. She juggled two part-time jobs to support herself. It wasn't easy, but it was what she really wanted to do.

After three years, she had steadily built up her community. She acquired paying sponsors for her blog, wrote a book on travel, and is now often paid to travel. Hotels want her to review their business for her blog, so they offer her a complimentary stay. Her next step is to start a travel touring company with her new husband, whom she met in her Meetup group! Of course, they both share a love of travel.

Jackie could not have built her business without following her bliss. Her enthusiasm attracted people who wanted to join her. Her passion gave her business the wings to fly. Jackie is an example of how a SEEKER finds a way to make her passion pay and her work play, because she won't settle for anything less.

THE SEEKER'S path sounds alluring. But when you follow your passion, you don't always have a road map and money is not guaranteed. THE SEEKER boldly walks into the unknown even if she is flying by the seat of her pants. She sees this as a grand adventure and wouldn't have it any other way.

THE SEEKER'S highest business potential is to be a Trailblazing Goddess. Here, she no longer hops from one thing to the next looking for answers, adventure or entertainment. She has grown wise from her journey and is centered in herself. Her wanderlust is balanced with real stability, both inner and outer. She is like a passionate gypsy who becomes a seer and the curious student who becomes a teacher. Instead of being a Trailblazer for her own purposes, she now inspires others along their path.

The Elephant in your Business
Magic in Commitment

To rock your Feminine Type, every woman needs to know when she has stayed at the ball too long—when the clock strikes midnight and her carriage turns back into a pumpkin. This is the point at which her strengths turn into her weaknesses.

Your carriage, SEEKER, turns back into a pumpkin when your need to explore takes over your business. You may not even realize this is happening. You are convinced you are focused on your business, but the truth is that you don't execute your brilliant ideas. You live to explore, grow and learn. You want a flow of fresh experiences to continually expand yourself. The last thing you would ever want to do is limit yourself, but this is exactly what can happen if you don't understand the elephant in your business.

The truth is, your lust for exploring can sidetrack you. There are times when getting sidetracked is valuable, because it can provide essential information that you need for your ultimate goals. But getting sidetracked can also block your momentum, tie up your money and end up limiting you in the end. Like getting caught in quicksand, your adventures can pull you farther and farther away from your goals. If you are continually hijacked you cannot bring your projects to fruition. If you spread yourself too thin, nothing gets the attention it needs to progress.

Getting sidetracked can block your momentum, tie up your money and end up limiting you in the end.

You can also get sidetracked when you don't commit to anything wholeheartedly. You may commit for a time, but then you can lose interest and back out. It takes persistence and commitment to build your business. Without them, you miss out on the gifts they could bring you such as money, recognition, security and ultimately the freedom you desire.

Follow your own Inner Compass

What you seek is seeking you. ~Rumi

Flexibility and adaptability are your strengths in your business. Your open-mindedness helps you to grow, learn, adapt and change. You have the ability to see a multitude of possibilities in every situation and you love to absorb wisdom from everyone and every experience. However, you have to be careful that you don't take this too far. The truth is, you can get lost if you look outside yourself for all your answers.

It can be comforting to have many resources in navigating your path. Life is complex and often it can feel overwhelming. However, there is a point at which you are not benefiting by absorbing the advice of others, but only giving your power (and money) away. If you need to consult with your life coach, your spiritual teacher, your astrologer, your energy healer, your yoga teacher and then do a green juice cleanse in order to find your clarity, you may be losing yourself in this process.

The problem is that your own inner compass spins wildly out of control when you ignore it. The more you need advice from others, the more you lose your own inner connection. Take a step back and center yourself. Check in with yourself first. You are your own ultimate guide—because your soul knows the way.

You are the ultimate guide you seek—because your soul knows the way.

Inspirations for THE SEEKER

I am rooted, but I flow. ~Virginia Woolf

The following inspirations can help you align with your highest business potential—The Trailblazing Goddess. The more you focus on creating these inner shifts, the more transformation and success you will see.

~ I enjoy the benefits of having an area of expertise in my business.

~ I stay focused on one goal and achieve it.

~ I know when it's time to explore and when it's time to plan for the future.

~ I listen to my own inner guidance and I trust it.

~ I let money work for me.

~ I complete my projects and experience the rewards of doing so.

~ I create a strong financial foundation to support my dreams.

~ I take pride in my accomplishments.

~ I notice if I am getting sidetracked and I refocus.

~ I harness the magic that comes from my commitment.

Wake Up Your Inner SEEKER

~Passion & Enthusiasm~

THE SEEKER knows that you rock your business when you love what you do. If your work doesn't inspire you, it won't inspire others. If you scored low on THE SEEKER, she has wisdom that can help you succeed.

- Happiness is an inside job and a lifelong commitment.
- Go with the flow. There is magic in it.
- The journey is just as important as the destination.
- Be true to yourself. Follow your bliss.
- Your enthusiasm is compelling and attractive.
- Make your passion pay by making your work play.
- Stay open-minded about what you can learn in every situation and from every person.
- Discover what is good about every experience.
- Your dreams matter, your happiness matters and your joy matters.
- Spontaneity is very productive.

14

The Leader
Biz Types

The Ambitious SUCCESS GIRL
&
The Bold DIVA

The Ambitious SUCCESS GIRL

Quick Look

QUALITIES: Driven, focused, positive, confident, motivational, influential, ambitious

BIZ TYPE: The Leader

BUSINESS POTENTIAL: The Inspirationista

SUPERPOWERS: Confidence and ambition

FASHION STYLE: The best of the best. Designer labels and accessories. Fine jewelry.

COMMUNICATION STYLE: Confident, positive, motivational

DISLIKES: Being seen as average or mediocre

MOTIVATION: Recognition, accomplishment, success

OUT OF BALANCE: The Materialist

Who's That Girl?

You get in life what you have the courage to ask for. ~Oprah Winfrey

The SUCCESS GIRL doesn't shrink her dreams to fit reality—she molds reality to fit her dreams. She wants her biggest, boldest and most outrageous dreams, and she is willing to take risks to get them. Her philosophy is that more is always much better. In everything she does, she wants to rise to the top. She dislikes the idea of being ordinary, average or like everyone else. She wants to shine in the spotlight.

Alive with possibility, THE SUCCESS GIRL brings a joy and enthusiasm to her work because it is her passion. She loves imagining the best possible scenarios for her life. She envisions her goals and believes she can accomplish them. She is a believer and an achiever.

Her Superpowers are her confidence and ambition. She knows how to move toward what she wants and manifest it. THE SUCCESS GIRL doesn't spend time in self-doubt. Why should she—she knows it's a waste of her creative potential. People are attracted to this quality in her and they want to know her secret. They have forgotten how to be powerful creators and THE SUCCESS GIRL reminds them that they are.

> *People have forgotten they are powerful creators and THE SUCCESS GIRL reminds them that they are.*

She works hard to make her dreams a reality, and no one can cram more into one day than she can. She is always on the go, crossing things off her checklist—and she has a long list. She is happiest when she's productive and accomplishing things.

THE SUCCESS GIRL is focused on making money and doesn't apologize for it—just like THE DIVA. They both put money front and center in their business. If they aren't making money, they change course. THE SUCCESS GIRL stays motivated to make money because she wants a certain lifestyle. She knows that money makes it all happen, so she's on top of it!

As a businesswoman, THE SUCCESS GIRL is constantly expanding. She loves gaining status, stature and even becoming a celebrity. Moving on to bigger and better things is always on her mind. She accomplishes her goals and then sets higher ones. She doesn't understand people who come to a comfortable plateau. She has an ambitious and competitive spirit.

> *She accomplishes her goals and then sets higher ones*

THE SUCCESS GIRL loves to be in the spotlight and this serves her very well in promoting her business. A master networker, she knows how to make powerful business contacts, create lucrative joint ventures and collaborate with others for even more business success. She actively seeks out business partners who can take her to greater heights.

THE SUCCESS GIRL'S highest potential is to become The Inspirationista. Here, her own personal success is no longer her sole objective because she has a larger vision. Her motivation is now about the contribution she can make—she is connected to her greater soul purpose. She has found her authentic self and it transforms her. She now uses her powerful ability to create and manifest to support others.

The Elephant in your Business

Happiness cannot be travelled to, owned, earned, worn or consumed. Happiness is the spiritual experience of living every minute with love, grace and gratitude. ~Byron Katie

The Zen of Success

You're always moving forward with confidence. You love your accomplishments and getting recognition for them. In this effort, you have only one obstacle to watch out for. You have to be careful that you don't push your stiletto to the metal in cultivating your image of success, because in this process you can lose something essential—yourself. This can happen because you think that the more success you have, the more valuable you will be—and the happier you will be. In this way you trade your true feelings in for your achieving, and your authentic self can get lost in the shuffle.

You know how to be successful. You know how to create outer success, but your journey to conquer the world must include your connection to your true self or you will never be satisfied.

~ LIZ ~

Feminine Type: THE SUCCESS GIRL/ EXCELLENCE GIRL
Biz Type: The Leader-Expert

Liz lived in her dream house. She had a beautiful family and worked as a business writer. She felt proud of herself, because she had everything she wanted in her life. She was a success, and she wasn't shy about letting people know it. In fact, she had a circle of friends who all felt proud of their well-positioned lives.

When the economy shifted in 2008, her husband's real estate empire crumbled and she lost her job. They had to sell their big house and move into a small apartment complex in a nearby town. Ironically, Liz had always driven by these same apartments thinking, "Thank God I don't live there." Those apartments were her worst nightmare, and now she was living in one of them.

To pour salt into this wound, her friends abandoned her. They didn't want to associate with her anymore. Distraught, Liz found her way to me for coaching. She had to reconcile all that had happened. I typed her as a SUCCESS GIRL/ EXCELLENCE GIRL.

During that time, she realized the small apartment she had never wanted to live in was actually just fine. She never thought she could be so happy without her elite lifestyle, but she had to admit that she was. She was happy because she was free to discover her authentic self. In her old life, she was too caught up in maintaining her image and status. Now, she was free to be herself.

As we worked on refocusing her writing business, Liz realized that she had been hiding her comedic talent and wanted to write a humorous blog. Soon, she began a quirky blog that rapidly gained followers. Liz became ambitious in a new way—eager to stay connected to her authentic self. She saw through the illusion of the image she had created and wasn't about to go back to it.

She shared with me that if the winds of fate hadn't shifted, she might never have found her authentic self or her true writing style.

The Zen of success is knowing that having more does not make you more, and having less does not make you less. Often your true purpose can come into better focus when you have less because you are not so distracted. Honor yourself enough to know that you are more than the sum of your success and achievements. Go for your big dreams, but let go of your attachment to them as proof of your worth and value. This will give you more space in your life for your authentic self and give your striving self a rest.

The Zen of success is knowing that having more does not make you more, and having less does not make you less.

Discover your Soul Purpose

Ask yourself what you *really* desire? What is underneath your drive for success? What do you really want? Consider that there is a powerful purpose driving you. You are who you are for a very specific reason. All your experiences in your life have contributed to the beautiful tapestry of who you are. There is not one thread out of place—not one! The flaws you perceive you have and the mistakes you feel you have made are all the threads of you. Trust your path. It has made you who you are.

When you honor all that you are, something unique and wonderful can happen. You realize that all you have learned over the years are the precious building blocks that reveal the real contribution you are here to make. When you are in touch with this, it becomes your soul purpose and all your success will be truly inspiring and fulfilling.

What do you really want? Consider that there is a powerful purpose driving you. You are who you are for a very specific reason.

Inspirations for THE SUCCESS GIRL

The following inspirations can help you align with your highest business potential—The Inspirationista. The more you focus on creating these inner shifts, the more transformation and success you will see.

~ I am enough right now.

~ I enjoy the journey, not just the destination.

~ I have the power to choose happiness now. It's my choice.

~ I tap into my soul purpose.

~ Having more doesn't make me more. Having less doesn't make me less.

~ I listen to my true feelings and emotions.

~ Success happens on many levels which can't always be measured by money.

~ Money and success do not have the power to define my value.

~ I nurture my authentic self.

~ I slow down so I can stay in touch and in tune with myself.

Wake Up Your Inner SUCCESS GIRL
~Confidence, Clarity & Certainty~

Your self-worth is determined by you. You don't have to depend on someone telling you who you are. ~Beyonce

THE SUCCESS GIRL knows that you rock your business when you have confidence, clarity and certainty. People are attracted to these qualities and want to be a part of your vision. If you scored low on THE SUCCESS GIRL, it's time to wake her up and make her your partner in success. Here is what you can learn from her:

- Continually expand your ideas for what is possible.
- Let money flow to you.
- If you are confident, your clients will be confident.
- Believe in yourself.
- You are a powerful creator, worthy of creating whatever you want.
- Don't give up when the going gets tough.
- Anticipate your upcoming successes.
- Bounce back from setbacks wiser and stronger than before.
- Don't underestimate the power of being possibility thinker.
- Think big and dream big.
- You are only limited by your own imagination.

The Bold DIVA

Quick Look

QUALITIES: Direct, authentic, extroverted, confident, protective, influential

BIZ TYPE: The Leader

BUSINESS POTENTIAL: The Global Transformer

SUPERPOWERS: Courage and charisma

FASHION STYLE: Big and bold

COMMUNICATION STYLE: Direct, commanding

DISLIKES: Having her authority questioned

MOTIVATION: Power, influence, authority

OUT OF BALANCE: The Steamroller

Who's That Girl?

The thing women have yet to learn is nobody gives you power. You just take it. ~ Roseanne Barr

THE DIVA is a self-possessed woman. She speaks up for what she needs and goes for what she wants. Sure, she may be seen as demanding, but THE DIVA is unapologetically herself. She goes where others fear to tread. Fearlessness and moxie are her gifts.

THE DIVA is known for her direct, tell-it-like-it-is attitude and voice. You never know what she is going to say. She follows *The Rebel's Handbook*, which says that she can (and should) stir the pot, kick up dirt, and kick some ass if need be. In a world full of Good Girls who go to acrobatic lengths to never offend anyone, THE DIVA is a breath of fresh air. She is 100 percent authentic. She tells the truth, even if it bothers people. She has diva-tude.

> *THE DIVA follows The Rebel's Handbook, which says that she can (and should) stir the pot, kick up dirt, and kick some ass if need be.*

Tough and uncompromising, she's the boss. She can't have people telling her what to do. THE DIVA needs to be the authority in her work environment. Her motto is, "My life, my rules."

Of all the Feminine Types, THE DIVA is the most at ease with herself—flaws and all. She accepts herself and doesn't change to please others. You can either love her or hate her, but rest assured she isn't spending time wondering what you think of her. She is free in a way that none of the other Feminine Types are. She doesn't apologize for being herself.

THE DIVA has an outgoing personality and easily makes influential connections in her networking. She loves people and she needs to socialize. People are often mesmerized by her self-confident presence and they recognize her as a leader.

Her Superpowers are her charisma and courage. This makes her a rule breaker and a ground shaker. She doesn't back down from challenges or obstacles—she pushes through, around or over them. THE DIVA often leaves her own unique mark on the world, forging new pathways by daring to do what no one has done before. In this way, she often leads the way for other women to follow.

> *THE DIVA often leaves her own unique mark on the world, forging new pathways by daring to do what no one has done before.*

THE DIVA owns her power and goes after what she wants. She is connected to her desires, and this is a large part of what makes her so powerful in manifesting them. Her power is in knowing what she wants and in not denying herself. Women are not always encouraged to stand in their power, command attention, be demanding or even have desires. If they do, they might be called a bitch or bossy. This doesn't bother THE DIVA. She is just being true to herself and she doesn't see a problem with that.

THE DIVA doesn't back down from what she wants or shrink herself to make others more comfortable. In this way, THE DIVA may appear to others as selfish. So herein lies the conundrum that many women find themselves in when they want to own their power and ambition—they fear that they will look selfish or self-centered or be called a bitch. This societal imprint dictates that the ideal, desirable women is selfless—she gives herself up to care for the needs and desires of others. Even though this may sound outdated, it is still very much a part of our collective consciousness.

Wise women know that it is not selfish to speak up and go for what they want. Every woman has an inner DIVA that awaits and deserves her full attention. It's the part of her that: tells her truth, doesn't back down and doesn't apologize or shrink her dreams and goals. This is not the DIVA who is imbalanced, but simply the woman who knows what is right for herself and stands her ground.

Every woman has an inner DIVA that awaits and deserves her full attention—the part of her that tells her truth, doesn't back down, doesn't apologize or shrink her dreams and goals.

As a businesswoman, THE DIVA has many gifts. The fact that she knows what she wants makes her a powerhouse of potential. Her courage to face obstacles helps her accomplish her goals. THE DIVA'S unabashed love of money is part of her magnetism. She pursues it and she may even choose her business based on its ability to yield a high income. She is unapologetic about focusing on profit, power and her ambitions.

THE DIVA'S highest potential is to be The Global Transformer. In this way, she uses her charisma and courage to effect positive change in the world. Here, her work is no longer about herself, but about the positive transformation she can create for others. She harnesses all her charisma to be a force for good on the planet. To get there, she has learned to work with people from her heart—to balance the polarities of power with love.

The Elephant in your Business

To conquer oneself is a greater task than to conquer others. ~Buddha

True Power

You have enviable business skills to accomplish what you want, but these skills only work if you know how to powerfully connect with people. Because you think in terms of power, your challenge is to balance your power with your vulnerability. This opportunity shows up in the relationship area of your business.

~ ANGELA ~
Feminine Type: THE SUCCESS GIRL/ DIVA
Biz Type: The Double Leader

Angela's Feminine Type was THE SUCCESS GIRL/ DIVA. She was a Double Leader Biz Type with a Nurturer shadow. She told me she suspected she might be driving people away in her sales business. I went to an event with her to observe her style of connecting with people. What I observed was that as soon as Angela said hello to people, she was selling herself. In fact, she went into full throttle sales mode. She gave her advice and did some name dropping to establish her authority as an expert.

It never works to make a conversation all about yourself and what you are selling. Even though Angela was passionate and focused, she was overwhelming people. She told me her sales style worked some of the time, but not most of the time. She didn't know what else to do.

I recommended that Angela borrow qualities from The Nurturers, because that was her Biz Type shadow. This included courting her potential clients by taking time to get to know them better, so she could develop a personal connection with them. When Angela pushed, her clients pulled back. It was hard for Angela to hear this, but she was willing to work differently.

She recognized she was pushing people away, so she went to work making changes. Her transformation included softening her brown and black power suits with some peach, blue and pink scarfs. In this way, she adopted an approachable fashion style from The Nurturers—THE SWEETHEART and THE SAINT. Angela loved this new softer look. She went to work being much more personable in all her conversations—no selling, just connecting.

Angela returned to her our next coaching session and told me that people were responding differently to her. She was now *reading their subtle cues and recognizing when she needed to be more invitational. When she did, she got better results.*

Before we started working together, Angela couldn't see how people were reacting to her. Now she was paying close attention to people. She was developing rapport and connection with her clients before she did any selling. Over time, these shifts created a profound transformation in her sales business.

THE DIVA might be the first to say that she isn't changing herself for anyone. But Angela was eager to modify her sales style. She had to have success in her business—she needed to make changes. The truth is we are sometimes more willing to make changes when we absolutely have to. As if on cue, Universal Intelligence has a way of conspiring to help us get out of our self-created ruts by bringing us the precise circumstances we need to do this.

> As if on cue, Universal Intelligence has a way of conspiring to help us get out of our self-created ruts by bringing us the precise circumstances we need to do this.

Angela told me no one had ever addressed these areas of her business, and she was grateful I did. She learned that true power is knowing when to be soft and when to be strong—she now knew she didn't have to overpower people to get their attention. She learned the power of connection.

Uplift Others & You Uplift Yourself

People admire your strength DIVA. Your charisma is undeniable, but with this gift comes a great responsibility. Make sure your power uplifts and validates the strengths of others, as well as yourself. People see you as a powerful leader already. You really don't have to be the queen bee in every conversation. If you insist upon it, it is a sure sign that you have become imbalanced. Your power is in learning to share the spotlight. When you encourage the people around you to shine brightly—you become a real star.

To enhance your status even more, use your charisma to create a ripple effect of positivity and camaraderie—uplift others. Knowing how to create harmony with your words and sharing the spotlight is the sign of your true strength.

When you use your charisma to support and uplift others, you uplift yourself as well. With this wind at your back, you will be unstoppable.

When you encourage the people around you to shine brightly—you become a real star.

The Leader Biz Types

Inspirations for THE DIVA

If you think the cause of your problem is out there, you'll try to solve it from the outside. Take the shortcut: solve it from within. ~Byron Katie

The following inspirations can help you align with your highest business potential—The Global Transformer. The more you focus on creating these inner shifts, the more transformation and success you will see.

~ I don't always have to be in charge.

~ I work in cooperation and collaboration with people.

~ I focus on building relationships.

~ I use my charisma to uplift others.

~ I value and appreciate feedback from others, and I let them know it.

~ I listen carefully to people.

~ I am aware of how people respond to me.

~ My real power is in being receptive and flexible.

~I relax my need to be the authority and take over.

~ I grow, adapt and change as needed.

~ I share the spotlight.

Wake Up Your Inner DIVA
~Strength to push through obstacles~

If you obey all the rules, you miss all the fun. ~Katharine Hepburn

THE DIVA knows that you rock your business when you have the courage to push through your obstacles. Without strength, you may give up. If you scored low on THE DIVA, you will want to know all her secrets. Here is what you can learn from her.

- Know what you want and then go for it 100 percent.
- Dare to shine.
- Being powerful is your birthright.
- Showing up and speaking up is not showing off. It is sharing your gifts.
- Trust that you have a powerful purpose, different from others, but no less powerful.
- Step into your greatness. There are people waiting for what you have to offer.
- Have the courage to claim your dreams.
- You have to break some rules to move out of your comfort zone.
- Expand your willingness to achieve what you want.
- Don't limit the amount of money you can make.
- Don't apologize for focusing on making money.
- Speak up and speak your truth.

15

Rock On with
The 4 Feminine Success Secrets

Evolve Yourself
Rock Your Intuition
Embrace Your Power
Befriend Your Shadow

With The Feminine Type Success System, you have gained the wisdom to rock your unique signature of feminine power and transform your business. You are no longer stuck repeating patterns that don't work. You have the tools and pathways necessary to take your business to the next level of success.

The last step on your yellow brick road is to gather up the four jewels that are scattered throughout this book—the Four Feminine Success Secrets. They are the keys that shift your mindset. With these secrets, you have everything you need to navigate your business in the direction you want.

The secrets are uniquely feminine because they tap into a woman's innate wisdom. For example, women understand that life is a continual process of growth. Women have an intimate connection to their bodies and intuition. Women know themselves as powerful creators and they understand the value and importance of accepting all the different parts of themselves. These strengths aren't often seen as powerful qualities in our culture, but they can serve you well in your business. Tap into your innate feminine wisdom and let it empower you.

Feminine Success Secret #1
Evolve Yourself

The first Feminine Success Secret is to keep evolving. Just like Dorothy in *The Wizard of Oz* was on a journey of self-discovery and self-mastery—so are you. Think of your business as your own yellow brick road. As Dorothy found out, it's about finding yourself and claiming all the different parts of yourself—*evolving*.

It is human nature to want to stay in our comfort zone, but as an entrepreneur, you must stretch yourself. This is what makes having your own business such a fantastic opportunity—you get to grow! When you do, you're wearing the ruby slippers and you have all the power.

When you evolve, your business evolves.

Feminine Success Secret #2
Rock your Intuition

The second Feminine Success Secret is to rock your intuition. Women are naturally intuitive and this is your lucky charm in business. Think of your intuition as the hotline to your soul.

For centuries women have been led to ignore their intuition in favor of their rational mind. Yet, there is no point in ignoring your intuition, just as there is no point in ignoring your rational mind. They work their best when they work together.

When you learn to listen to your inner voice, it can become your greatest asset in your business. Your intuition is actually a very practical tool that can help you in a multitude of ways. The more you validate your intuition by listening to it, the clearer your connection to it becomes.

It is important to know that if something doesn't feel right to you—stop and listen! You need no further proof than your own gut feeling—none whatsoever! Your inner knowing is sufficient.

Your Intuition is the hotline to your soul.

Feminine Success Secret #3
Embrace Your Power

The third Feminine Success Secret is to embrace your power as a creator. There are times in your business when you may be tempted to give up or blame others for what feels like your bad fortune—don't! When you feel like a victim, you lose your power and your potential to create what you want.

Just like Dorothy met her scarecrows, tin men, lions, wizards and both good and wicked witches, you will too. Your obstacles are part of your path. Learn from them and let them empower you.

A powerful creator pays attention to what she can learn in every situation—letting all her experiences strengthen and enlighten her. With this mindset, she discovers that there is something good in every situation and she looks for it.

If that victim feeling tries to sneak up on you, pick up your magic wand and create the reality you want instead—because you can! Challenges appear to teach you something vital, not to turn you into a victim. The dragons you slay garner you wisdom—wisdom you will eventually pass on to others.

> *Challenges appear to teach you something vital, not to turn you into a victim.*

Feminine Success Secret #4
Befriend Your Shadow

The fourth Feminine Success Secret is to befriend your shadow. Your shadow is a part of you that you are not owning, claiming or using. In fact, you may even be rejecting this part of yourself. Yet, your shadow contains essential qualities that can benefit your business success. Think of your shadow as unclaimed gifts—and you definitely want to claim your gifts!

When you befriend your shadow, you gain the power you need to move into the highest potential of your Feminine Type. The beauty of The Feminine Type Success System is that is shows you where your shadow is.

As Glinda the Good Witch said to Dorothy, "You've always had the power. You just had to learn it yourself."

> *Think of your shadow as unclaimed gifts—and you definitely want to claim your gifts!*

Conclusion

You now have the secrets to put your crown on and rock your business like the queen that you are. If you get to a fork in the road and the signs aren't clear, you can come back to The Feminine Type Success System. It will assist you in navigating your direction or in helping you make a course correction, all by banking on your feminine strengths.

It can help you:

- Rock your Feminine Type
- Rule your Biz Type(s)
- Reclaim your power from your shadow
- Rock on with The Four Feminine Success Secrets

Afterword

To find coaching, trainings and resources for Rock Your Feminine Type To Rock Your Business, visit www.rockyourfemininetype.com.